D1614127

Canadian Culinary
Olympic Chefs
Cook at Home

Canadian Olympic Culinary Chefs Cook at Home

First Printing July 2012

Library and Archives Canada Cataloguing in Publication

Canadian Culinary Olympic chefs cook at home / [prepared by the] Alberta Culinary Arts Foundation.

(Canada cooks series)

Includes index.

ISBN 978-1-927126-24-0

1. International cooking. 2. Cookbooks. I. Alberta Culinary Arts Foundation II. Series: Canada cooks series

TX725.A1C383 2012   641.59   C2011-908559-3

Special thanks to Chef's Hat Inc. for supplying props for the front cover.

Published by

Company's Coming Publishing Limited

2311 – 96 Street

Edmonton, Alberta, Canada T6N 1G3

Tel: 780-450-6223   Fax: 780-450-1857

www.companyscoming.com

Company's Coming is a registered trademark owned by Company's Coming Publishing Limited

We acknowledge the financial support of the Government of Canada through the Canada Book Fund for our publishing activities.

Printed in China

CONTENTS

About the World Culinary Olympics

Culinary Team Canada (see page 154)

The World Culinary Olympics, held every four years, is the largest and most prestigious culinary competition in the world. The 2012 competition is being held in October in Erfurt, Germany—and Culinary Team Canada is going for gold!

Canadian culinary teams have competed internationally since 1972, but 1984 marked the "coming of age" of Canada's chefs—the year that they were crowned world champions and established themselves as worthy Olympians in the international culinary arena. Canada was also declared world champions in 1992, and has been awarded gold several times.

At the World Culinary Olympics, national teams—comprising five members, one backup member and one manager—strive to obtain the highest number of total points to win best overall and receive world champion distinction. They use the indigenous foods and flavours of their home country, and are judged by their peers in two specific competitive categories: Restaurant of Nations Hot Competition (66 2/3 points) and Cold Display Table Competition (33 1/3 points).

Working in full view of judges, team members are scrutinized as they prepare an elaborate three-course dinner for 100 people in only five hours. A gold medal performance demands concentration, physical stamina and composure from each individual member as well as superior teamwork. Innovation must be balanced with viability when the team creates competition entries. Judging is based on harmony of competition, appetizing and elegant presentation, and correct basic culinary preparation using modern techniques, indigenous products and exemplary plating.

Introduction

The members of Culinary Team Canada are among the finest chefs in the world. They have trained for years to develop and hone their craft. They practise again and again to ensure that every recipe is complete and that every bite is nothing short of perfect. They compete against world-class chefs from every corner of the globe.

And at the end of every day, the members of Culinary Team Canada have to come home and cook for themselves and their families.

Cream of Wild Rice Soup, p. 38

Well, that's easy for them, you might be thinking. *They know what they're doing; they're professional chefs!*

Yes, they're professional chefs, but they face the exact same challenges that you face in your kitchen: dealing with picky eaters, considering food allergies and sensitivities, discovering at the last second that there's no more sugar in the pantry, planning weekly menus and going grocery shopping, needing to throw something together in a hurry because the kids need to get to hockey and soccer, making sure the family eats healthily, cooking for a large crew over the holidays, hunting through the fridge and freezer to see what they can whip up tonight...

Sound familiar? That's the thought behind *Canadian Culinary Olympic Chefs Cook at Home*—these Olympic-calibre chefs cook at home for their families just like everyone else does. In this book, they have collected some of their favourite dishes to prepare at home. Some, like Tortilla Rolls with Cream Cheese, Walnuts and Olives or Manitoba Corn Soup, come together quickly and with only a handful of ingredients. Others, like Roasted Beef Tenderloin in a Box, provide an unexpected and dramatic presentation suggestion. Many recipes would be perfect for a special occasion, such as Sidney Island Rack of Venison with Saanich Blackberry Glaze. These are at-home, everyday recipes with a gourmet spin.

So What's Different?

Perhaps the biggest difference when you're a professional chef is that you don't get invited out for dinner very often—which is unfortunate, because chefs love to eat and share food with friends just like everyone else!

Because they work with food on a daily basis, chefs tend to be more conscious about what they—and their families—eat. They try to eat less processed food and focus instead on fresh, healthy alternatives. Many believe in the local foods movement, buying and using ingredients that are grown and produced locally. Many chefs get to know the farmers and producers in their area (often within 100 miles) and want to support them. There are innumerable wonderful Canadian producers of meat, fish, fruits, vegetables, dairy products and more. You can get to know local producers yourself by visiting farmers' markets and talking with the vendors. Many grocery stores also stock local and Canadian ingredients.

Roasted Duck with Blueberry Sauce, p. 100

Professional chefs also tend to be a bit more adventurous in their home cooking than some of the rest of us. You might be at a loss for how to use chanterelle mushrooms or spot prawns or duck—but professional chefs aren't, and they've told you exactly how to in this book! They make use of ingredients that you might have skipped over or avoided in the past. Try them out—you might discover some new favourites!

Chefs have a lot of experience perfecting making their dishes *look* every bit as good as they taste. Because chefs cook for a living, the people they are feeding tend to have high expectations of their dishes—both in taste and appearance. You can use the photographs in this book as inspiration for plating your dishes and experiment

with other presentations as you gain confidence in your ability. Here are a couple tips from the pros:

• Try using white plates to serve your food. You don't want your dishes to be competing with your food—you want your food to be the main event! Simple white dishes provide a clean and elegant background.

• Use a touch of garnish to give your dishes a finished and polished appearance. Try a dollop of whipped cream on a creamy soup, sprigs of rosemary and thyme with grilled meat, or lightly sautéed tomatoes and vegetables to add colour with fish or a risotto.

Your food will have a restaurant-quality look before you know it!

About the Ingredients

The recipes in this book were written by many different chefs, each of whom have their own favourite ingredients. That's why you might find kosher salt in one recipe and sea salt in another. You can feel free to substitute your own favourites.

There are many different places that you can acquire the ingredients used in this book. Of course, there's your local grocery store. If it doesn't carry what you're looking for, you can always ask a manager if it's possible to bring in what you need.

Farmers' markets are a good source for fresh produce and meat. Often specialty grocery stores and health food stores carry a wide variety of spices and other ingredients. But if you're having trouble finding an ingredient, try ordering it online! Many professional chefs do this all the time—it's fast and convenient, and you can acquire virtually any ingredient you need from anywhere in the world.

Here are some general notes on ingredient choices that we've found to be successful. You'll also find notes about specific ingredients sprinkled throughout this book.

Bay Leaves—Fresh leaves are occasionally available at large grocery stores and can be specially ordered. In a well-sealed container in the fridge, they can last three or four months.

Butter—Use unsalted. Butter is easiest to measure using the convenient markings on the wrapping.

Citrus Juices—Lemon juice, lime juice and orange juice are best fresh squeezed.

Coconut Milk—Use unsweetened coconut milk in cans. Naturally sweet, it is often better than cream in savoury dishes.

Eggs—Use large, free-run eggs. They should be at room temperature for baking.

Flour—Unbleached all-purpose flour is a good choice.

Garlic—Use fresh garlic. It really does make a difference!

Herbs—Use fresh herbs whenever possible. The best alternative to fresh herbs is frozen, not dried. You can freeze herbs yourself in the summer when they are plentiful, or you can find them in the freezer section of some better grocery stores.

Mushrooms—Morels and chanterelles can be found in the wild, but we advise that you confirm the identification of mushrooms with an experienced collector before cooking them. Some species of mushrooms are acutely toxic and can cause death.

Mustard—Use good quality mustard for everything from sandwiches to dressings to sauces. When the last few teaspoons of mustard cling to the bottom of the jar, add fresh lemon juice, olive oil, sea salt and fresh pepper; shake and use as a salad dressing.

Pepper—Peppercorns that you grind yourself have much better flavour than pre-ground pepper.

Salt—Brings out the flavour in food. Sea salt, kosher salt, Celtic salt...choose a favourite or obtain some of each. Using a better-quality salt means that you will use less, because the flavour is more intense. If you wish to reduce your salt intake further, use fresh herbs, various spices and flavour-lifters such as lemon juice—these will help maintain the flavour intensity while reducing the salt content.

Dark Chocolate Espresso Mousse with Raspberries, p. 148

Star Anise—This strongly anise-scented spice is sold dried as quarter-sized, star-shaped clusters of 5 to 10 pods, each containing a single seed. The seeds can be used on their own, crushed or ground, or the entire stars can be added, then removed before serving.

Stocks—Make homemade stocks whenever you can. Your best substitute for homemade are the good-quality stocks that are available in tetra paks. Miso, a fermented soybean paste, is another interesting alternative to stock, and it will keep in the refrigerator for several months. Stir it in 1 Tbsp (15 mL) at a time until you have a rich, full flavour.

Sugar—Organic, unrefined sugar is considered healthier than white, bleached sugar. When looking for a rich brown sugar, try muscovado sugar, available in grocery and health food stores. It still contains the minerals and vitamins originally in the sugar cane plant, and it has a full molasses flavour.

Vinegar—Apple cider vinegar has a great flavour when you need an all-purpose vinegar. Balsamic vinegar has a great flavour in everything from soups to sweets.

Yeast—Unless otherwise specified, use regular dry yeast; 1/2 oz (15 g) is equal to 1 Tbsp (15 mL) fresh yeast.

Making the Most of this Book

Often, when chefs cook at home, they don't follow a recipe. They might see a picture that looks good and then try to recreate it, adding a little of this and a little of that—or their meal might depend entirely on what was on sale at the grocery store that week and what's left over in the fridge! So when chefs give you a recipe, they've had to be very deliberate about writing it down. The next time they make it, it might be completely different!

This book features 72 recipes written by current and former members of Culinary Team Canada. They're some of the Olympic chefs' favourite recipes to cook at home for themselves and their families. But the chefs feel free to change up the recipes when the inspiration strikes, and so should you. Make substitutions based on what you like and what you have available. You don't need to be a slave to a recipe. If the recipe calls for 1 Tbsp of sugar and you want more (or less), add more! If you don't like Swiss cheese, use the cheddar that you already have in your fridge. You'll develop your own instincts as you cook—follow them. And of course, use the recipes given here as tested-and-true guidelines.

The recipes in this book were contributed by many different chefs, and all of them have different preferences for measuring ingredients. Some prefer to use volume measurements (i.e., 1 cup [250 mL] diced celery); others favour weight measurements (i.e., 4 oz [113 g] corn); others employ a combination of both. You may find it helpful to invest in a small kitchen scale.

Most chefs cook because it's what they love to do. Food is love. And that's the moral of this story—follow your own inspiration and do what you love.

You may occasionally come across an ingredient or cooking method that you're unfamiliar with. We've described several of them throughout this book (for example, see "How to Shuck an Oyster" on page 9), and you can check our website, **companyscoming.com**, for more tips.

How to Shuck an Oyster

Gather oysters, an oyster knife and a clean dish towel. Place oyster, cupped-side down, on a dish towel. Fold towel over the rounded edge of the oyster, leaving the more acute edge visible. Place your left palm on top of the towel and oyster; then, using the oyster knife, work the point of the blade into the pointiest edge to create a separation between the top and bottom shell.

Slide the edge of the blade just underneath the top (flat) side of the oyster to separate the meat from the shell.

At this point, you can discard the top half of the shell.

Slide the knife along the bottom to separate the meat from the shell. The oyster should now be free in the shell.

Fresh Fanny Bay Oysters with Double-smoked Bacon and Shallot Vinaigrette

Serves 8

6 x 1 oz (28 g) slices double-smoked bacon, cut into ¼ inch (6 mm) cubes

2 shallots, minced

1 garlic clove, minced

6 Tbsp (100 mL) dry white wine

3 Tbsp (45 mL) white balsamic or champagne vinegar

juice and zest from 2 lemons

Worcestershire sauce to taste

salt and pepper to taste

16 fresh Fanny Bay oysters, shucked (see page 9)

lemon wedges and hot sauce for garnish

Render bacon over medium so that fat is released but bacon does not brown. Reduce heat slightly and add shallots and garlic. Cook until aromatic and softened, then deglaze with wine. Reduce by half, remove pan from heat and add vinegar, lemon juice and zest, Worcestershire sauce, salt and pepper. Set aside at room temperature.

Place shucked oysters on salt bed and generously spoon vinaigrette over top. Garnish with fresh lemon and hot sauce on the side.

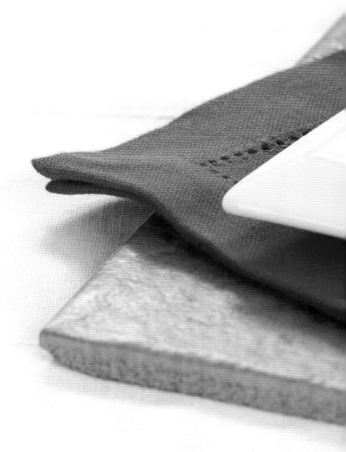

Oysters need to be scrubbed thoroughly with a brush to remove any dirt or debris. Store them resting, cupped-sides down on a piece of crumpled foil, in fridge until needed.

Fried Clams with Avocado Dip

Serves 4

Fried Clams

2 cups (500 mL) corn flour

½ tsp (2 mL) salt

¼ tsp (1 mL) white pepper

1 Tbsp (15 mL) fine yellow cornmeal

1 can (355 mL) beer

1 Tbsp (15 mL) granulated sugar

1 egg

20 large Quahog clams, shucked (see page 9)

canola oil for deep frying

Avocado Dip

1 avocado

½ cup (125 mL) sour cream

⅓ cup (75 mL) cream cheese

juice from 1 lime

In a shallow bowl, stir together corn flour, salt, pepper and cornmeal. Pour half of mixture into another shallow bowl. In a separate bowl, whisk together beer, sugar and egg until well combined.

Heat oil in deep fryer or high-sided saucepan to 365°F (185°C). Dredge clams in first bowl of flour mixture, then dip in beer mixture, then toss in second bowl of flour mixture. Shake off excess, then fry until clams turn golden. Season with salt.

Combine all ingredients in a blender and purée. Serve fried clams with avocado dip.

Pacific Dungeness Crab and Chive Soufflé Cakes with Ricotta and Citrus

Serves 4

Soufflé Cakes

8 oz (225 g) fresh Dungeness crabmeat, shelled

pinch *each* of sea salt and freshly ground black pepper

zest from 2 lemons, 1 lime and 1 orange

¼ oz (7 g) minced chives plus whole stems for garnish

6 whole eggs

3¼ cups (800 mL) whole-wheat flour

Place crabmeat in a glass bowl and check thoroughly that there are no shell pieces in the meat. Add salt, pepper, lemon zest, lime zest, orange zest, chives and eggs. Mix thoroughly. Add flour and mix well with a spatula.

Preheat oven to 375°F (190°C). Pour mixture into flexipan muffin moulds and bake for 12 to 15 minutes until wooden pick inserted in centre of cake comes out clean. Cakes will rise a bit. Transfer to wire rack to cool.

(continued on next page)

In a stainless steel bowl, mix ricotta, citrus juices, garlic and wine.

To serve, remove crab soufflé cakes from pan and place on plate. Spoon about 2 Tbsp (30 mL) ricotta mixture next to crab cake. Garnish with chive stems and fresh citrus zest.

Ricotta and Citrus

6 oz (170 g) ricotta cheese

1½ tsp (7 mL) citrus juices (juice from lemons, lime and orange)

¾ tsp (4 mL) minced garlic

1½ tsp (7 mL) white wine

Salt and Pepper Squid with Togarashi Dip

Serves 4

Squid

1 lb (500 g) baby squid, cleaned

½ box purchased tempura batter

⅓ cup (75 mL) all-purpose flour

1 tsp (5 mL) sea salt

1 tsp (5 mL) freshly ground black pepper

peanut or canola oil for deep-frying

½ lime

1 jalapeño, sliced paper thin for garnish

¼ bunch cilantro, chopped

Togarashi Dip

3 Tbsp (45 mL) mirin

1½ Tbsp (25 mL) rice wine vinegar

1 cup (250 mL) mayonnaise

1 Tbsp (15 mL) togarashi spice

1 Tbsp (15 mL) soy sauce

1½ Tbsp (25 mL) chopped pickled ginger

salt and pepper to taste

Set aside squid tentacles. Slice tubes into nice-sized rings and pat dry with paper towel.

Make tempura according to package directions. Season flour with salt and pepper; set aside.

Heat oil in a deep fryer or high-sided saucepan to 350°F (175°C). Toss squid rings and tentacles in seasoned flour and shake off excess. Dip into tempura and then fry for 1 to 2 minutes until lightly golden. Drain on paper towel and season with salt and pepper.

To finish, toss with fresh squeeze of lime, sliced jalapeño and cilantro. Serve with togarashi dip.

For togarashi dip, combine mirin with vinegar in a small saucepan; bring to boil and reduce to a syrup. Allow to cool and add mayonnaise, togarashi, soy sauce and ginger; season to taste with salt and pepper.

Togarashi, or Shichimi togarashi, *is a Japanese spice blend that includes red chili powder, sichuan pepper, roasted orange peel, white and black sesame seed, hemp seed, nori and ground ginger. It is available at most Asian markets.*

Seared Qualicum Scallops with Fennel and Golden Beet Salad with Grapefruit

Serves 8

Grapefruit Dressing

juice and zest from grapefruit used in the salad

juice and zest from 1 lemon

1 shallot, minced

4 tsp (20 mL) agave nectar

4 tsp (20 mL) Dijon mustard

salt and pepper to taste

7/8 cup (200 mL) extra-virgin olive oil

Fennel and Golden Beet Salad

2 fennel bulbs, thinly sliced crosswise

1 golden beet, julienned

1/2 red onion, julienned

1 grapefruit, segmented

Scallops

4 tsp (20 mL) canola or grape seed oil

16 Qualicum scallops

salt and black pepper to taste

juice of 1 lemon

4 tsp (20 mL) cold butter

juice of 1/2 grapefruit

Combine all dressing ingredients except oil in a blender and mix. While mixing, slowly add oil in a steady stream until emulsified.

Combine salad ingredients with grapefruit dressing, then toss. Let stand overnight to allow flavours to develop.

Heat a 12 inch (30 cm) heavy-bottomed sauté pan over high; add oil. The pan is at the right temperature when oil shimmers and is almost smoking. (If oil begins to smoke, remove pan from heat and allow to cool for 1 to 2 minutes before searing scallops).

Pat scallops dry and season with salt and pepper. Place only 8 scallops in pan at a time; do not overcrowd. Caramelize for 1 to 2 minutes before lowering heat to medium. Turn scallops over and continue cooking for 1 minute. Remove from pan and cook remaining scallops in same manner; when done, put first batch back into pan with the rest and drizzle lemon juice over scallops. Add butter and allow butter to melt completely. Remove scallops from pan and pour grapefruit juice and butter sauce over top. Serve with salad.

Scallops benefit greatly from the caramelizing created during the searing process. The surface browning helps to highlight the natural sweetness of scallops and seals in the flavour and moisture that might otherwise be lost.

Baked Baby Tomato, Basil and Goat Cheese Tart with Aged Balsamico

Serves 4

2 onions, sliced

4 tsp (20 mL) olive oil

salt to taste

1¼ cups (300 mL) chicken stock

2 tsp (10 mL) white wine vinegar

1 sprig of fresh thyme, leaves picked off

4 x 4 inch (10 cm) discs of puff pastry

20 red and yellow cherry tomatoes

¼ cup (60 mL) extra-virgin olive oil, plus extra for drizzling

sea salt to taste

7 oz (200 g) softened goat cheese

1⅔ cups (400 mL) balsamic vinegar

kosher salt to taste

8 to 10 basil leaves, cut in chiffonade for garnish

Sauté onions slowly in oil for around 30 minutes and season with salt. Add chicken stock and vinegar and simmer for about 30 minutes, stirring occasionally, until pan is dry and onions are golden. Add thyme leaves.

Preheat oven to 400°F (200°C). Par-bake puff pastry according to package directions, then scoop out centre. Bake a second time until very lightly golden. Set aside.

Dip cherry tomatoes into boiling water for 10 to 15 seconds until skins just loosen and tomatoes are still firm. Cool and peel tomatoes, then toss with extra-virgin olive oil and sprinkle with sea salt.

Whip goat cheese until light.

Over medium, reduce balsamic vinegar by about 80% until slightly thickened.

To assemble the tarts, spread 2 heaping Tbsp (30 mL) soft goat cheese on bottom of baked pastry. Spoon 1 heaping Tbsp (15 mL) onion mixture on top. Top with a single layer of peeled cherry tomatoes. Bake in a 450°F (230°C) oven for 7 to 10 minutes until golden brown and hot. Remove from oven, sprinkle with kosher salt and drizzle with extra-virgin olive oil. Spoon balsamic reduction onto plate and place warm tart in centre, then sprinkle with basil.

Wild Mushroom and Goat Cheese Ravioli with Arugula and Red Pepper Relish

Serves 4 as an appetizer

Pasta Dough

2¼ lbs (1 kg) all-purpose flour, plus extra flour for rolling

7 whole eggs

1 Tbsp (15 mL) kosher salt

⅓ cup (75 mL) water

¼ cup (60 mL) olive oil

Wild Mushroom Filling

¼ cup (60 mL) vegetable oil

2 shallots, finely minced

1 lb (500 g) wild mushrooms (morels, chanterelles, pines, etc.)

pinch *each* of kosher salt and freshly ground black pepper

3 oz (85 g) goat cheese

Red Pepper Relish

1 cup (250 mL) finely diced roasted red peppers (canned is okay)

1 Tbsp (15 mL) sugar

¼ cup (60 mL) orange juice

1 tsp (5 mL) kosher salt

1 tsp (5 mL) white wine vinegar

⅛ tsp (0.5 mL) sambal oelek

Place dough hook on mixer; combine all pasta dough ingredients in mixer on low. Mix for 2 minutes on medium. Turn off and check that all ingredients are coming away from sides. Mix for 4 more minutes. Take out of mixer and wrap in plastic. Refrigerate overnight.

For wild mushroom filling, heat oil in a sauté pan over high until hot. Add shallots and mushrooms quickly. Sauté for 2 minutes while stirring constantly. Turn heat to low, and cook until mushrooms are reduced by half and slightly caramelized. Stir in salt and pepper. Transfer mushrooms to a bowl and cool in fridge. When ready to assemble ravioli, mix goat cheese into mushroom mixture.

Add all red pepper relish ingredients to a saucepan; cook over high for 1 minute. Turn down to low, and cook until relish thickens in consistency. Remove from heat and cool.

(continued on next page)

To assemble ravioli, take pasta dough out of fridge and cut into smaller pieces so it will roll through pasta roller. Roll to very thin (see Tip), or last setting on roller (usually 6). Roll 2 sheets of pasta dough. Cover with plastic wrap while rolling remaining dough.

Brush egg wash onto rolled pasta dough, and place 1 Tbsp (15 mL) mushroom mixture about every 2 inches (5 cm). Cover with other sheet of pasta dough. Press down around pockets containing mushroom mixture. Cut around pockets with any shaped cutter. Make sure ravioli is airtight and sealed.

Boil a saucepan of water. Reduce heat to a simmer; add ravioli and cook for 2 minutes. Drain, transfer to a bowl and toss with butter, salt and pepper. Place on plate with red pepper relish and arugula leaves. Crack more pepper on top if you like.

Tip

Hand-roll the pasta if you do not have a pasta roller.

Ravioli

egg wash of 1 egg yolk mixed with 2 Tbsp (30 mL) water

butter for tossing cooked ravioli

salt and pepper to taste

2 oz (57 g) arugula leaves

Tortilla Rolls with Cream Cheese, Walnuts and Olives

Makes 5 to 6 rolls

2 cups (500 mL) Philadelphia-style cream cheese, room temperature

¼ cup (60 mL) salted butter, room temperature

⅓ cup (75 mL) finely diced red pepper

⅓ cup (75 mL) coarsely chopped green olives

¼ cup (60 mL) chopped walnuts or almonds

¼ cup (60 mL) minced chives

salt and pepper to taste

5 to 6 medium tortillas (regular or whole wheat)

thinly sliced smoked salmon (optional)

Beat cream cheese and butter until smooth. Sauté red pepper for 30 seconds in a buttered frying pan; drain well. Add to bowl with olives, red pepper, nuts, chives, salt and pepper. Beat until well mixed.

Spread mixture generously and evenly on tortillas. Top with smoked salmon if desired. Roll firmly, wrap in plastic, and twist ends to tighten. Place in freezer (to make cutting rolls easier). Take out of freezer 1 hour before serving.

To serve, cut into slices ½ inch (12 mm) thick or more. Display on a platter. Serve chilled.

Thin slices of smoked salmon atop the cream cheese mixture add a festive touch. You could also add a little local blue cheese, grated old Cheddar cheese or a few drops of spicy sauce to the mixture.

Olive Bread

Makes 12 slices

⅔ cup (150 mL) dry white wine

⅔ cup (150 mL) canola oil

4 eggs

2 cups (500 mL) all-purpose flour

2 tsp (10 mL) baking powder

1 tsp (5 mL) salt

½ lb (225 g) ham, cut into small cubes

⅞ cup (200 mL) green olives in oil, halved

⅞ cup (200 mL) black olives in oil, halved

⅞ cup (200 mL) grated Gruyère cheese

butter

Preheat oven to 425°F (220°C). Mix wine, oil and eggs; beat well. Add flour, baking powder and salt; beat to blend. Add ham, olives and cheese. Mix well.

Lightly butter a rectangular cake or bread pan. Dust with flour and shake off excess. Pour bread mixture into mould. Let rest at room temperature for 15 minutes.

Bake for 45 minutes until a wooden pick inserted in centre comes out dry. Slice and serve warm with tomato or bell pepper coulis, or cut into bite-sized squares and serve cold or at room temperature with an aperitif.

Well covered in plastic wrap, this bread keeps 8 to 10 days in the refrigerator.

Corn Butter Lobster Stew

Serves 4

Corn Butter

3½ oz (100 g) minced onion

3½ oz (100 g) corn, freshly shucked or frozen

2 sprigs of fresh thyme

⅞ cup (200 mL) white wine

1¼ cups (300 mL) light lobster stock or prawn stock

⅔ cup (150 mL) diced butter

Lobster Stew

1 cup (250 mL) sliced young leek (white and light green parts only)

4 oz (113 g) corn, freshly shucked

12 asparagus tips, cut on the bias

11 oz (310 g) lobster meat, cut into large pieces

4 baguette slices, toasted with butter

4 pancetta slices, grilled or baked until crisp

2 cherry tomatoes, quartered

4 sprigs of fresh dill

For corn butter, sweat onion, corn and thyme in a hot pot. Add wine and lobster stock and simmer for 5 minutes. Remove from heat and remove thyme. With an immersion blender, carefully purée liquid, then add butter slowly until creamy. Use caution when blending hot liquids. Strain, season and keep warm.

For stew, sauté leek, corn and asparagus in sauté pan for 2 to 3 minutes until softened but not browned. Add corn butter and lobster. Heat until lobster is just cooked.

Transfer stew to serving dish or individual bowls and garnish with baguette, pancetta slices, cherry tomatoes and dill.

Land and Sea Chowder

Makes 4 cups (1 L)

1 oz (28 g) diced bacon

½ oz (14 g) butter

1 garlic clove, minced

2 oz (57 g) diced onion

2 oz (57 g) diced celery

2 oz (57 g) diced carrot

1½ oz (43 g) flour

⅓ lb (150 g) mussels, well scrubbed and beards removed

⅓ lb (150 g) clams

3 cups (750 mL) fish stock

2 oz (57 g) red potato, diced

2 oz (57 g) chanterelle mushrooms, sliced

½ cup (125 mL) corn juice

2½ oz (70 g) scallops

6 Tbsp (100 mL) heavy cream

salt and pepper to taste

Cook bacon to render fat, leaving enough fat for a roux. Add butter and sauté garlic, onion, celery and carrot. Add flour and cook until incorporated into a roux.

Meanwhile, steam mussels and clams until shells open. Discard any that do not open. Remove meat from shells; drain and reserve meat and mussel liquid separately. Add reserved liquid and fish stock to roux mixture; stir gently to incorporate.

In a separate pot, cook potato until fork-tender. Drain and add to fish stock.

Meanwhile, sauté chanterelles in a small amount of butter and add to fish stock with corn juice; simmer to incorporate flavours. Add scallops to sauté pan and cook for 2 minutes per side.

Finish chowder with seafood and cream just before serving. Heat through and season with salt and pepper.

Mussel Soup with Avocado, Tomato and Cilantro

Serves 4

$1\frac{1}{2}$ lbs (680 g) washed leek, thinly sliced (white and pale green parts only)

2 Tbsp (30 mL) butter

4 sprigs of fresh thyme

2 cups (500 mL) dry white wine

$1\frac{1}{2}$ cups (375 mL) water

3 lbs (1.4 kg) mussels, well scrubbed and beards removed

1 cup (250 mL) whipping cream

$\frac{1}{4}$ tsp (1 mL) *each* salt and coarsely ground white pepper

1 firm, ripe avocado

20 small grape tomatoes, cut into quarters

3 Tbsp (45 mL) chopped fresh cilantro

salt and pepper to taste

Cook leek in butter in a large pot over medium, stirring occasionally, until soft. Add thyme and cook for about 1 minute. Stir in wine and water, then increase heat to medium-high and bring to a boil. Add mussels and cover pot. Cook just until mussels are open, then transfer mussels to a large bowl. Discard any that do not open.

Working over a bowl, remove mussel meat from shells and put into bowl. Pour any cooking liquid from mussels back into pot. Pour cooking liquid through a fine-mesh sieve and into a clean saucepan. Add cream, salt and pepper, then heat over low until hot. Stir in mussels and heat until just warmed through.

To serve, halve avocado and, with a large spoon, separate skin from avocado. Cut into $\frac{1}{2}$ inch (12 mm) cubes, and then toss gently with tomatoes and cilantro in a bowl. Season with salt and pepper to taste. Ladle $\frac{1}{2}$ cup (125 mL) soup into 4 warm soup bowls. Then spoon avocado tomato mixture onto rims or sides of bowls.

Olive Oil-poached Salmon Soup with Baby Vegetables and Tomato Chutney

Serves 4

Poached Salmon

1 nori sheet, julienned

4 x 4¼ oz (125 g) salmon fillets

3 cups (750 mL) olive oil

2 oz (57 g) fresh basil, cut in chiffonade

1½ oz (43 g) fresh thyme leaves

3½ oz (100 g) diced shallot

salt and pepper to taste

Tomato Chutney

3½ oz (100 g) julienned white onion

¾ oz (21 g) minced red pepper

1 shallot, minced

3 Tbsp (45 mL) olive oil

¼ cup (60 mL) raspberry vinegar

¼ cup (60 mL) sugar

13 oz (370 g) peeled, seeded and chopped tomatoes

salt and pepper to taste

Sprinkle nori over salmon. Wrap in plastic and refrigerate overnight.

Combine oil, basil, thyme and shallots in a small pot. Using a thermometer, bring oil to 140°F (60°C) and hold it at this temperature. Cook salmon in olive oil for 15 minutes until it feels firm to the touch. Remove from oil; pat dry and set aside.

For tomato chutney, sweat onion, red pepper and shallot in olive oil. Add vinegar and sugar and reduce by 75%. Add tomato and simmer until liquid has evaporated and chutney is deep red in colour. Taste and adjust seasoning.

(continued on next page)

Toss pea sprouts with oil, salt and pepper.

Place chives in a blender with oil and blend for 5 minutes on high. Strain through cheesecloth or fine-mesh strainer. Season to taste. Refrigerate until ready to use.

Blanch vegetables and place in a bowl. Slice potatoes lengthwise and blanch; add to bowl. Sprinkle with salt and pepper.

Simmer fish stock and remove from heat; whisk in butter.

To serve, spoon vegetables into bowls, and pour stock mixture over top immediately. Top with poached salmon and then a large spoon of tomato chutney on top of fish. Add pea tendrils and drizzle with chive oil before serving.

Pea Tendrils

3 oz (85 g) pea sprouts

extra-virgin olive oil to taste

salt and pepper to taste

Chive Oil

3 oz (85 g) chopped chives

½ cup (125 mL) olive oil

salt and pepper to taste

Baby Vegetables in Broth

2 cups (500 mL) baby vegetables (e.g., squash, carrots, fennel and spring onion)

1 cup (250 mL) baby fingerling potatoes

salt and pepper to taste

1⅔ cups (400 mL) fish stock

3½ oz (100 g) butter

Buttercup Squash Velour

Serves 10

1 Tbsp (15 mL) butter

2 carrots, peeled and sliced

2 buttercup squashes, peeled and diced

1 large Yukon gold potato, peeled and diced

1 medium cooking onion, peeled and diced

1 leek, washed and sliced (white and light green parts only)

5 cups (1.25 L) chicken stock

pinch of nutmeg

salt and pepper to taste

$\frac{1}{2}$ cup (125 mL) whipping cream

$\frac{1}{4}$ cup (60 mL) maple syrup

In a medium pot, heat butter over medium and soften carrots, buttercup squashes, potato, onion and leek for about 15 minutes. Add chicken stock, nutmeg, salt and pepper; simmer for 15 minutes.

Remove from heat and allow to cool, uncovered, for about 2 minutes. Transfer to blender and carefully purée until smooth. Use caution when blending hot liquids. Return to stove and heat and adjust seasonings. Finish with cream and maple syrup.

Tip

To add a deeper flavour to the soup, roast the buttercup squash instead of cooking it with the other vegetables.

Cream of Wild Rice Soup

Serves 6

2½ oz (70 g) diced onion

2 Tbsp (30 mL) canola oil

2 oz (57 g) diced celery

2 oz (57 g) diced carrot

3½ oz (100 g) sliced mushrooms

2 Tbsp (30 mL) flour

6 cups (1.5 L) chicken stock, divided

⅓ lb (150 g) cooked wild rice

salt and pepper to taste

⅔ cup (150 mL) whipping cream

Sauté onion in oil until slightly translucent. Add celery, carrot and mushrooms; sauté on low for 3 to 4 minutes. Add flour and stir until dry; cook for 2 minutes. Add half of chicken stock and bring to a boil while stirring constantly. Soup will start to thicken.

Add remaining chicken stock and wild rice; simmer for 30 minutes on low. Season with salt and pepper.

Heat up cream and add it to soup. Simmer for 3 minutes and serve.

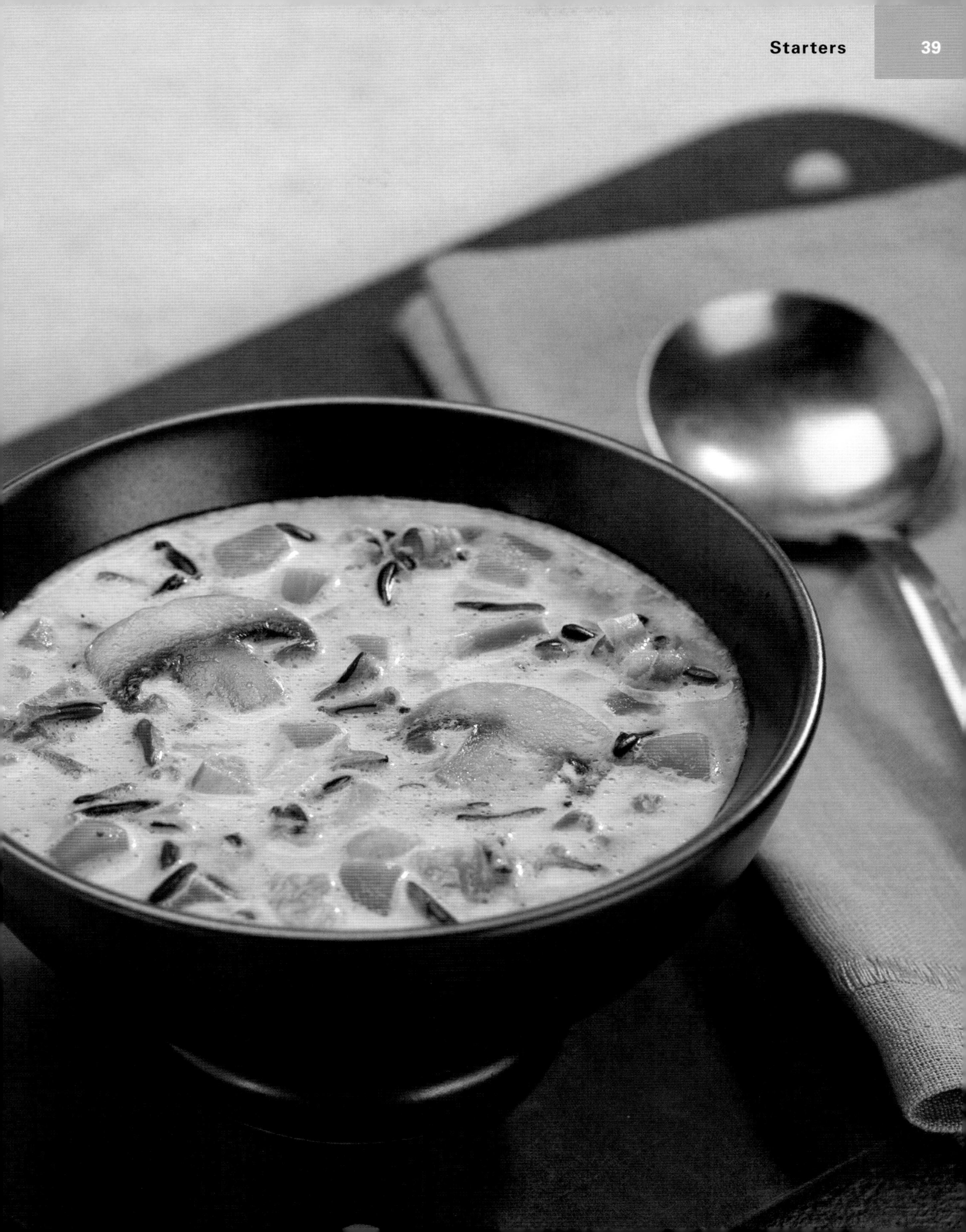

Great Northern White Bean Soup with Gorgonzola

Serves 8

2 tsp (10 mL) canola oil

3½ oz (100 g) diced onion

3 garlic cloves, finely chopped

3½ oz (100 g) diced celery

3½ oz (100 g) diced carrot

2½ oz (70 g) sliced mushrooms

4 cups (1 L) chicken stock

⅞ cup (200 mL) seeded and diced tomato

⅓ cup (75 mL) uncooked orzo pasta

11 oz (310 g) precooked Great Northern white beans

¼ cup (60 mL) chopped, cooked spinach

1 Tbsp (15 mL) chopped basil

1 Tbsp (15 mL) chopped flat leaf parsley

salt and pepper to taste

3 oz (85 g) crumbled Gorgonzola cheese

Heat oil and sauté onion, garlic, celery, carrot and mushrooms until softened. Add chicken stock, tomato, orzo and beans. Simmer for 20 minutes over low.

Add spinach, basil and parsley. Season with salt and pepper.

Place a small amount of Gorgonzola in the middle of each bowl and pour piping hot soup over cheese.

Great Northern beans are related to kidney and pinto beans. They are usually somewhat cream-coloured.

Manitoba Corn Soup

Serves 6

1 lb (500 g) Yukon gold potatoes

1 lb (500 g) onions

¼ lb (113 g) butter

2 lbs (900 g) corn, freshly shucked

8 cups (2 L) chicken stock (approximately)

salt, pepper and lemon juice to taste

2 cups (500 mL) whipping cream

Peel potatoes and onions and roughly chop. Heat butter in a large pot and add chopped potatoes and onions; lightly sauté. Add corn. Add enough chicken stock just to cover ingredients. Bring to a simmer and cook until potatoes are tender.

Transfer to blender and carefully purée until smooth. Use caution when blending hot liquids. Return to pot; season with salt, pepper and lemon juice. Finish with cream and serve.

Asparagus Vichyssoise with Tarragon

Serves 4

2 Tbsp (30 mL) butter

1 cup (250 mL) washed, thinly sliced leek (white and pale green parts only)

½ cup (125 mL) peeled, cubed Yukon gold potatoes

2½ cups (625 mL) chicken stock

3 cups (750 mL) trimmed asparagus, cut into 1 inch (2.5 cm) pieces

salt and pepper to taste

¼ cup (60 mL) whipping cream

1 Tbsp (15 mL) finely chopped fresh tarragon

Melt butter in a large saucepan over medium-high. Add leek and potato; sauté for 2 minutes. Add chicken stock and bring to a boil. Reduce heat to medium and cook until vegetables are tender, about 10 minutes. Add asparagus, but reserve 8 asparagus tips for garnish. Simmer until asparagus is just tender, about 5 to 6 minutes depending on thickness of stalks. Remove saucepan from heat.

Transfer soup to blender (or use an immersion blender) and carefully purée until smooth. Use caution when blending hot liquids. Season with salt and pepper. Refrigerate soup until chilled.

In a small bowl, whisk cream, tarragon and a dash of salt until cream is slightly thickened. Divide soup among 4 shallow bowls. Drizzle tarragon cream over soup and garnish with reserved asparagus tips.

White Asparagus Soup

Serves 6

3 small onions, chopped

3 Tbsp (45 mL) butter

4 cups (1 L) clear chicken broth

2 lbs (900 g) white asparagus, trimmed and cut into 1 inch (2.5 cm) pieces

2 cups (500 mL) peeled, diced potatoes

⅛ tsp (0.5 mL) white pepper

½ cup (125 mL) whipping cream

minced chives for garnish

In a large saucepan, sauté onions with butter. Add broth, asparagus, potatoes and pepper. Bring to a boil. Reduce heat; cover and simmer for 20 minutes until vegetables are soft.

Transfer soup to blender and carefully process until smooth. Use caution when blending hot liquids. Return to pan. Add cream and cook over low until heated through. Ladle into serving bowls and sprinkle with chives.

Chicken, Savoy Cabbage and Barley Soup

Makes 8 cups (2 L)

1 Tbsp (15 mL) butter

2 cups (500 mL) sliced Savoy cabbage, ribs removed

½ cup (125 mL) sliced leek (white and pale green parts only)

½ cup (125 mL) sliced carrot

½ cup (125 mL) chopped onion

6 cups (1.5 L) chicken stock

2 Tbsp (30 mL) pearl barley

1 to 2 chicken legs

salt and pepper to taste

1 Tbsp (15 mL) minced chives

croutons made from a baguette (see Tip)

Heat butter in stock pan and sauté cabbage, leek, carrot and onion. Add chicken stock, barley and chicken and bring to a boil. Cook over medium for about 1 hour until barley and chicken are cooked.

Transfer chicken to work surface. Let cool slightly. Remove skin and bone, and cut meat into cubes; return to soup. Taste for seasoning and sprinkle with chives.

Serve piping hot with croutons.

Tip

To make croutons, cube slices of baguette, toss with some olive oil and bake until somewhat crunchy.

Barbecued Duck Consommé

Serves 6

Duck Stock

1 whole barbecued duck (reserve breast meat for garnish)

18 cups (4.5 L) water

1 onion, chopped

2 carrots, chopped

2 celery ribs, chopped

8 shiitake mushrooms, chopped

6 garlic cloves, minced

6 green onions, chopped

1¾ oz (50 g) ginger

6 star anise

½ cinnamon stick

½ tsp (2 mL) crushed white pepper

2 bay leaves

liquid from the barbecued duck

Soup

⅓ cup (75 mL) diced onion

⅓ cup (75 mL) diced carrot

⅓ cup (75 mL) diced celery

½ cup (125 mL) diced shiitake mushrooms

1 lb (500 g) ground pork

7 egg whites

10 sprigs of cilantro

Place all duck stock ingredients except duck breast meat in a large stock pot; bring to a simmer over medium. Reduce heat to a very light simmer and continue to cook for 4 hours. Strain stock and allow to cool; refrigerate overnight.

Combine onion, carrot, celery and mushrooms in a food processor and pulse until combined. Mix processed vegetables with pork and egg whites. Place into a tall, narrow stockpot with 12 cups (3 L) duck stock and bring to a slow simmer over medium-low, stirring constantly. Allow to cook until a hole forms in centre—do not boil. Gently simmer. Strain through cheesecloth.

(continued on next page)

For garnish, lightly sauté carrot, celery, corn, mushrooms and peas in oil. Arrange nicely in individual bowls. Top with sliced duck. Season soup to taste and ladle into bowls; garnish with green onion and cilantro.

Garnish

1 carrot, sliced on an angle

1 celery rib, cut on an angle

9 baby corn cobs, split in half

6 shiitake mushrooms, sliced

9 snap peas, cut into diamond shapes

1 Tbsp (15 mL) sesame oil

thinly sliced barbecued duck breast meat

2 green onions, sliced on an angle

12 small sprigs of cilantro

BC Albacore Tuna Tataki with Watercress, Endive and Grapefruit Salad and Ponzu Dressing

Serves 4

1 lb (500 g) BC albacore tuna

6 Tbsp (100 mL) vegetable oil, divided

salt and pepper to taste

1 oz (28 g) togarashi spice (see page 17)

⁷⁄₈ cup (200 mL) ponzu, divided

juice from 1 lime, divided

1 cup (250 mL) watercress

1 endive

1 grapefruit

1 Tbsp (15 mL) honey

Cut tuna into long loins, approximately 1 inch (2.5 cm) wide. Lightly coat with oil and season with salt, pepper and togarashi spice. Heat remaining oil in a non-stick pan on high. Sear tuna loins quickly on each side until outside is golden brown. Take care; you want the centre to stay raw while creating a nice sear on the outside.

Place loins in a shallow tray and drizzle with 3 Tbsp (45 mL) ponzu and half of lime juice. Cover with plastic wrap and refrigerate for 1 to 2 hours. Rotate tuna loins every 30 minutes to allow even marinating.

Wash watercress and place in bowl lined with paper towel to dry. Keep only the nicer leaves on the stems; discard any woody stems and leaves. Wash endive and cut off bottom core to loosen leaves. Peel leaves off endive and julienne crosswise, creating moon-shaped slices. Place grapefruit on cutting board and peel away all skin and pith. Carefully segment grapefruit with paring knife. Reserve all liquid for dressing. Reserve segments for salad.

To make ponzu dressing, mix together honey, remaining ponzu, remaining lime juice and reserved grapefruit juice, and season to taste with salt and pepper.

Give tuna a final turn in marinade and transfer to cutting board. Slice tuna and arrange on each of 4 plates.

Mix watercress and endive together in a bowl. Dress with ponzu dressing and season with salt and pepper. Arrange salad on plates and garnish with grapefruit segments.

Ponzu is a citrus sauce that is light yellow, tart and watery in consistency.

BC Spot Prawn Salad with Baby Spinach, Arugula and Shaved Fennel with Wasabi Vinaigrette

Serves 4

4 cups (1 L) water

juice from 1 lemon

2 bay leaves

6 Tbsp (100 mL) white wine

10 whole peppercorns

16 BC spot prawns

Wasabi Vinaigrette

2 tsp (10 mL) wasabi paste

1 Tbsp (15 mL) honey

6 Tbsp (100 mL) rice wine vinegar

$\frac{7}{8}$ cup (200 mL) vegetable oil

3 Tbsp (45 mL) sesame oil

salt and pepper to taste

Puffed Wild Rice

$1\frac{2}{3}$ cups (400 mL) vegetable oil

$1\frac{1}{2}$ oz (40 g) wild rice

salt and pepper to taste

Place water, lemon juice, bay leaves, wine and peppercorns in a large saucepan; bring to a simmer. Turn off heat and add spot prawns. Poach for 5 minutes until fully cooked. Transfer prawns to a plate and discard cooking broth. Allow prawns to cool for 10 minutes. Carefully peel (save prawn shells for prawn stock) and refrigerate. Prawns can be kept in fridge for up to 2 days.

For wasabi vinaigrette, whisk wasabi paste, honey and vinegar in a bowl. Slowly pour oils into bowl, whisking until emulsified. Season with salt and pepper. Refrigerate until ready to use.

For puffed wild rice, preheat oil in a deep fryer or small high-sided pot to 400°F (200°C). Add wild rice; remove when rice has puffed to top of oil. Transfer to paper towels to drain. Season with salt and pepper.

(continued on next page)

Toss all salad ingredients in a large bowl and add wasabi vinaigrette to taste. Place salad decoratively in 4 serving dishes and garnish each with 4 spot prawns and puffed wild rice.

Salad

2 cups (500 mL) baby spinach, picked and washed

1 cup (250 mL) baby arugula, picked and washed

1 small fennel, thinly shaved

10 cherry tomatoes, cut in half

1 baby cucumber, shaved

Crabapple and Brussels Sprouts Salad

Serves 2

Dressing

2 cups (500 mL) apple juice

1 cup (250 mL) white wine vinegar

1½ cups (375 mL) sugar

2 sprigs of thyme

Salad

½ cup (125 mL) lardons (double-smoked whole bacon cut into pieces)

1 cup (250 mL) cooked, cooled and quartered Brussels sprouts

1 cup (250 mL) crabapples, cut into wedges

canola oil to taste

salt and pepper to taste

candied pecan pieces

Place apple juice, vinegar, sugar and thyme in a pot. Reduce until it has the consistency of light syrup.

Cube lardons and cook until slightly crispy.

Toss Brussels sprouts, crabapples and lardons together with dressing, a little canola oil, salt and pepper. Garnish with candied pecan pieces.

This salad can be served warm or cold.

Braised Vancouver Island Beef Short Ribs with Natural Reduction

Serves 4

Short Ribs

$^7/_8$ cup (200 mL) vegetable oil, divided

2 lbs (900 g) boneless beef short ribs (see Tip), cut into 4 portions

salt and pepper to taste

1 onion, diced

1 carrot, peeled and diced

4 garlic cloves

2 cups (500 mL) red wine

8 cups (2 L) chicken stock

2 black cardamom pods

2 star anise

1 cinnamon stick

10 black peppercorns

1 bay leaf

Natural Reduction

$^7/_8$ cup (200 mL) rice wine vinegar

$3^1/_2$ oz (100 g) sugar

1 sprig of thyme

Sautéed Mushrooms

6 Tbsp (100 mL) vegetable oil

1 shallot, diced

30 chanterelle mushrooms, cleaned

10 morel mushrooms, cut in half and cleaned

3 Tbsp (45 mL) white wine

3 Tbsp (45 mL) butter

salt and pepper to taste

Drizzle $^1/_4$ cup (60 mL) oil on ribs and season with salt and pepper. Heat remaining oil over medium-high, and sear until golden brown. (Sear in batches if pot is not big enough.)

Remove meat from pot. Sear onion, carrot and garlic until golden brown. Deglaze pot with wine and reduce until almost dry. Place short ribs back in pot and cover with chicken stock. Add cardamom, star anise, cinnamon, peppercorn and bay leaf and simmer for 3 hours.

Remove short ribs and place in a small pot with $^7/_8$ cup (200 mL) braising liquid. Season remaining braising liquid with salt and pepper and reserve, keeping warm.

For natural reduction, heat rice wine vinegar and sugar in a pot over high and reduce by 75%. Add reserved warm braising liquid and reduce by another 75%. Strain through a fine-mesh strainer; sauce should have a slightly thick consistency. If sauce is not the right consistency, thicken it with a cornstarch slurry (equal parts cold water and cornstarch mixed in a small bowl). Add thyme and steep for 5 minutes before straining sauce one final time. Set aside.

For mushrooms, heat oil on medium in a large sauté pan. Add shallots and cook until translucent. Turn heat to high and add all mushrooms; sauté for 1 minute. Add wine and butter and sauté for 1 minute. Season to taste with salt and pepper.

(continued on next page)

Boil potatoes in salted water; simmer for 15 to 20 minutes until fork-tender. Mix milk and butter together. Drain potatoes and transfer to a bowl. Add milk mixture. Mash potatoes and beat further, adding milk if needed to achieve desired consistency. Add truffle oil. Taste for seasoning. Place in a pot and keep warm.

Place tomatoes and oil in a large pan and season with salt. Place pan in a 450°F (230°C) oven for 5 minutes until tomato skin starts to blister. Serve immediately.

Serve short ribs with reduction sauce, sautéed mushrooms, potatoes and tomatoes.

Tip

You can buy boneless beef short ribs, or just remove the bones yourself.

Truffled Potato Purée

4 large yellow nugget potatoes, peeled and cut into large squares

½ tsp (2 mL) salt

⅞ cup (200 mL) warm milk

3 Tbsp (45 mL) butter, melted

4 tsp (20 mL) truffle oil

Roasted Baby Tomatoes

8 cherry tomatoes

4 tsp (20 mL) olive oil

pinch of sea salt

Braised Chuck Flat Stroganoff

Serves 4

4 x 9 oz (255 g) beef chuck flat iron steaks

sea salt and black pepper to taste

2½ tsp (12 mL) extra-virgin olive oil

1 cup (250 mL) diced onion

⅔ cup (150 mL) sliced carrot

⅔ cup (150 mL) sliced celery

1½ cups (375 mL) sliced leek (white part only)

2 garlic cloves, smashed

2 cups (500 mL) red wine

5 cups (1.25 L) beef stock

2 bay leaves

3 sprigs of thyme

Pappardelle Pasta

1 lb (500 g) dry pappardelle pasta

extra-virgin olive oil as needed

Cream Sauce

2½ Tbsp (37 mL) butter

9 oz (255 g) diced onion

1 lb (500 g) button mushrooms, sliced

1 bay leaf

6 sprigs of thyme

3 cups (750 mL) whipping cream

salt and white pepper to taste

⅓ cup (75 mL) sour cream

juice from ½ lemon

Preheat oven to 275°F (140°C). Season beef with salt and pepper. Heat an ovenproof pot over medium and add oil. Sear beef on all sides until nicely browned. Add onion, carrot, celery, leek and garlic; cook for 1 to 2 minutes. Deglaze with wine and cook until liquid is evaporated. Add beef stock, bay leaves and thyme. Cover and braise in oven for 2 to 3 hours. Check beef after 2 hours; it should be soft and tender when cooked. To test, push on a piece and it should give but not fall apart; you may need to add extra stock depending how long the meat cooks.

When beef is cooked, allow it to cool in the liquid to keep it moist.

Blanch pappardelle according to package directions, but undercook it a little; you will be sautéing it to finish. Cool on baking sheet drizzled with a little oil.

For cream sauce, add butter and onions to a large stockpot over medium. Cook until clear. Add mushrooms, bay leaf and thyme. Cook mushrooms until all liquid is cooked out. Add cream and reduce by half. Season to taste with salt and pepper; remove from heat. Add sour cream and lemon juice. Allow sauce to cool. Remove bay leaf.

(continued on next page)

In another larger sauté pan over medium, add butter and oil. Allow to heat for 1 minute. Add shallots and mushrooms and cook for 2 to 3 minutes. Add cooked pasta and toss. Cook for 1 to 2 minutes; add cream sauce but do not boil. Season to taste with salt and pepper. Remove from heat and add fresh tarragon.

To serve, plate pasta and sauce. Top with beef; finish beef with coarse sea salt.

To Finish

¼ cup (60 mL) butter

2 Tbsp (30 mL) extra-virgin olive oil

75 thinly sliced shallot rings

1 lb (500 g) cremini mushrooms, cut into ¼ inch (6 mm) slices

course sea salt, white pepper and fresh tarragon to taste

Roasted Beef Tenderloin in a Box

Serves 8

Potatoes

5 Yukon gold potatoes, sliced into ¼ inch (6 mm) rounds

1 onion, peeled and sliced

5 garlic cloves, peeled

¼ cup (60 mL) olive oil

Beef Tenderloin

1 Tbsp (15 mL) canola oil

5 garlic cloves, peeled and minced

3 sprigs of rosemary, stemmed and chopped

3 to 5 sprigs of thyme, stemmed and chopped

1 x 6 lb (2.5 kg) whole AAA beef tenderloin, cleaned

1 Tbsp (15 mL) freshly cracked black pepper

1 Tbsp (15 mL) sea salt

1 small bunch of rosemary

1 small bunch of thyme

¼ cup (60 mL) vegetable oil

rosemary sprigs and thyme sprigs for garnish

Preheat oven to 400°F (200°C). Mix potatoes, onion, garlic and oil in a medium roasting pan, and roast in oven for about 15 minutes until potatoes begin to soften.

Line a pre-soaked wooden wine box with foil. Remove potatoes from roasting pan and arrange them in box; set aside.

Mix oil with garlic, rosemary and thyme, and rub all over beef. Season with pepper and salt. Tie beef with butcher's twine and weave bunches of rosemary and thyme underneath twine.

In a large sauté pan, heat oil over high. Place beef in pan and sear on all sides.

Place beef in box over potatoes; cover with foil. Set on a sheet pan, place in oven and roast until desired doneness. This dish is best served medium-rare (145°F [63°C]), about 60 to 70 minutes. For rarer, cook to 140°F (60°C); for medium, 160°F (71°C); for medium-well, 165°F (74°C); and for well done, 170°F (77°C). Remove from oven and set box aside for 15 minutes to allow meat to rest.

Remove foil and transfer meat to cutting board. Slice beef tenderloin, garnish with rosemary and thyme and serve over potatoes in wine box.

∾ *This dish is ideal for a dinner where you are looking for a wow factor! Note that the wooden wine box must be soaked in water for at least 2 hours before cooking.*

Veal Chops with Morel Sauce

Serves 6

3 Tbsp (45 mL) butter, divided

1 Tbsp (15 mL) minced shallot

1 Tbsp (15 mL) minced garlic

1 lb (500 g) fresh morel mushrooms, cleaned and halved

1 Tbsp (15 mL) parsley, chopped

6 thick-cut veal chops (milk-fed veal is best)

2 cup (500 mL) flour, seasoned with salt and pepper

1 Tbsp (15 mL) vegetable oil

½ cup (125 mL) Armagnac (a French brandy)

1 Tbsp (15 mL) Dijon mustard

3 to 4 Tbsp (45 to 60 mL) crème fraîche

kosher salt and freshly ground pepper to taste

Heat 2 Tbsp (30 mL) butter in a large sauté pan over medium. Sauté shallots and garlic for 2 minutes. Add morels and sauté for about 3 minutes until tender. Add parsley and set aside.

Preheat oven to 375°F (190°C). Dredge veal chops in flour and shake off excess. Heat oil and butter in a large ovenproof sauté pan over high. Sear chops for 3 to 4 minutes per side until golden brown. Transfer to oven for 5 to 6 minutes to finish cooking. Transfer chops to a plate.

Deglaze pan with Armagnac. Add Dijon mustard and stir to incorporate. Add crème fraîche, morel mixture and any juices from the resting chops, and bring to a simmer. Adjust seasoning with salt and pepper to taste. Serve veal chops with morel sauce.

Fraser Valley Pork Tenderloin, Okanagan Sour Apple and Port Wine Caramel, Yam Purée, Spinach and Crispy Onion Rings

Serves 4

Barbecue Lacquer

¼ cup (60 mL) vegetable oil, divided

1 Tbsp (15 mL) minced shallots

1 Tbsp (15 mL) minced garlic

¼ cup (60 mL) honey

1 tsp (5 mL) Dijon mustard

1 Tbsp (15 mL) molasses

pinch *each* of ground cinnamon, ground cayenne pepper, freshly ground black pepper, paprika, celery seed and turmeric

juice and zest of 1 lemon and 1 orange

Tenderloin

2 lbs (900 g) pork tenderloin, cut into 4 portions

2 Tbsp (30 mL) kosher salt

1 Tbsp (15 mL) freshly ground black pepper

1 Tbsp (15 mL) vegetable oil

Sour Apple and Port Wine Caramel

2 green apples

2 Tbsp (30 mL) olive oil

1 Tbsp (15 mL) minced shallot

2 Tbsp (30 mL) brown sugar

¼ cup (60 mL) port wine

For barbecue lacquer, add oil, shallots and garlic to a saucepan over medium. Sauté for 1 minute until shallots and garlic are translucent. Add honey, mustard and molasses. Turn heat to low and add all spices and juices. Cook for 2 more minutes. Remove from heat and set aside.

For tenderloin, preheat oven to 350°F (175°C). Rub pork with salt and pepper. Heat ovenproof sauté pan on high. Add oil and sear pork on all sides. Transfer to oven and cook for 5 minutes, then check for doneness. Remove from oven and let meat rest. Apply lacquer with brush over entire surface of pork.

For apple caramel, cut each apple into 8 wedges (with no seeds). In small saucepan on medium, add oil and shallots. Add apples and sauté for 30 seconds. Add brown sugar and port. Reduce until all apples are caramelized and still a bit firm, but do not overcook.

(continued on next page)

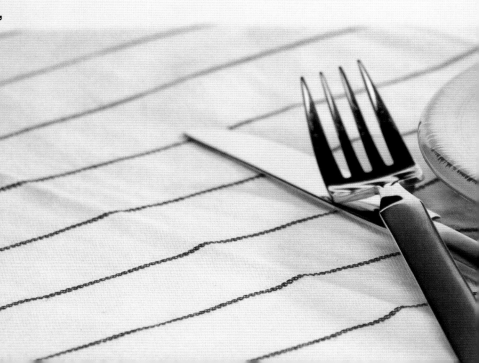

Cook yam in boiling water for 5 minutes. Drain and transfer to blender with chicken stock and a pinch of salt and pepper. Purée until smooth.

For onion rings, preheat oil in saucepan to 350°F (175°C). Using a mandoline, carefully slice onion very thinly. Add to milk in a bowl and soak for 10 minutes. Take onion slices out of milk and shake excess off. Dredge in flour then place in hot oil; fry for 1 minute until golden brown. Take out and drain on paper towel.

To serve, place 1 Tbsp (15 mL) yam purée on each plate. Sauté spinach quickly in butter and place next to yam purée. Cut pork tenderloin and place on plate. Add apples as shown. Garnish with crispy onion rings.

Yam Purée

2 cups (500 mL) peeled and diced yams

½ cup (125 mL) chicken stock

salt and pepper to taste

Crispy Onion Rings

4 cups (1 L) vegetable oil

1 white onion

1 cup (250 mL) 2% milk

½ cup (125 mL) all-purpose flour

To Serve

1 bunch baby spinach leaves, washed and stemmed

¼ tsp (1 mL) salted butter

Spiced Pork Tenderloin with Leek and Apple Cider Sauce and a Pear and Raisin Chutney

Serves 4

2 garlic cloves, diced

1 Tbsp (15 mL) grated ginger

¼ cup (60 mL) canola oil

2 Tbsp (30 mL) Chinese five spice

2 whole pork tenderloins, cleaned

salt and pepper to taste

Leek and Apple Cider Sauce

1 cup (250 mL) diced leek (white and light green parts only)

2 Tbsp (30 mL) butter

¼ cup (60 mL) apple cider

¾ cup (175 mL) chicken stock

⅔ cup (150 mL) heavy cream

1 tsp (5 mL) grainy mustard

2 tsp (10 mL) butter

1 Tbsp (15 mL) chopped parsley

salt and pepper to taste

Rub garlic, ginger, oil and Chinese five spice on tenderloins. Let rest, covered, in fridge overnight.

Preheat oven to 350°F (175°C). Season pork with salt and pepper, and pan-sear on all sides until golden brown. Transfer to oven and cook until it reaches an internal temperature of 138°F (59°C). Let rest for 6 minutes.

For sauce, sauté leek in butter in a small pot. Add apple cider and chicken stock; simmer until liquid is reduced by half. Add cream and mustard, and reduce by half again. Stir in butter and add parsley. Season to taste with salt and pepper; set aside.

(continued on next page)

Simmer chutney ingredients in a small pot until syrupy.

Serve pork with leek and apple cider sauce and pear and raisin chutney.

Pear and Raisin Chutney

6 oz (170 g) diced pear

1 oz (28 g) diced apple

2$\frac{1}{2}$ oz (70 g) peeled, seeded and diced tomato

1 oz (28 g) diced onion

1 oz (28 g) raisins

1$\frac{1}{2}$ tsp (7 mL) orange zest

juice from 1 orange

3$\frac{1}{2}$ oz (100 g) sugar

$\frac{1}{4}$ tsp (1 mL) cinnamon

$\frac{1}{4}$ tsp (1 mL) nutmeg

$\frac{1}{4}$ tsp (1 mL) cayenne

$\frac{1}{3}$ oz (10 g) grated ginger

$\frac{1}{4}$ cup (60 mL) white wine vinegar

pinch of saffron

Sloping Hills Organic Bone-in Pork Loin with Risotto

Serves 8

3 lbs (1.4 kg) pork loin, bone-in

salt and pepper to taste

olive oil for coating

Local Corn and Smoked Boerenkaas Risotto

2 ears corn, freshly shucked

1 white onion, diced

2 garlic cloves, minced

3 Tbsp (45 mL) olive oil

2 cups (500 mL) carnaroli rice

$\frac{2}{3}$ cup (150 mL) white wine or apple juice

chicken stock as needed

3 Tbsp (45 mL) butter

$3\frac{1}{2}$ oz (100 g) smoked Boerenkaas or Gouda cheese, grated

salt and pepper to taste

Preheat oven to 350°F (175°C). Pat pork dry, then season with salt and pepper and coat with oil. Place pork in a roasting pan that can also be used on stovetop. Roast for 15 minutes to caramelize surface of pork; reduce oven temperature to 225°F (110°C) and continue to cook until an internal temperature of 145°F (63°C) is reached.

Remove pork from pan, cover loosely with foil and allow to rest for 15 to 20 minutes before slicing.

Using roasting pan that pork was cooked in, sauté corn, onion and garlic in oil until soft. Add rice and continue to sauté until rice is completely coated with fat and is lightly toasted. Deglaze with wine and add chicken stock slowly, in $\frac{7}{8}$ cup (200 mL) intervals, until rice has reached desired texture, usually in about 15 to 20 minutes. Once rice is cooked, add butter and cheese and adjust seasoning.

To serve, slice pork and serve with risotto.

Whole roasted meats make for great fall meals. Corn is also at its finest in the fall; take advantage of its natural sweetness to make a rich risotto that highlights the mild sweetness in the organic pork. Add your favourite local medium-bodied cheese for depth and flavour without overpowering the pork.

Pork Belly with Creamy Polenta

Serves 6

1 lb (500 g) pork belly

salt and pepper to taste

Stewed Mushrooms and Vegetables in Sauce

$\frac{1}{3}$ oz (10 g) butter

3$\frac{1}{2}$ oz (100 g) diced onion

2 oz (57 g) diced celery

2 oz (57 g) diced mushrooms

healthy pinch of salt

6 Tbsp (100 mL) demi glace or veal jus

Polenta

butter for sweating off vegetables

2 oz (57 g) finely chopped carrots

1 tsp (5 mL) finely chopped shallots

1$\frac{1}{2}$ Tbsp (25 mL) finely chopped garlic

salt and pepper to taste

1$\frac{1}{3}$ cups (325 mL) milk

$\frac{2}{3}$ cup (150 mL) cream

2$\frac{1}{4}$ oz (63 g) cornmeal

3 oz (85 g) Parmesan cheese

1$\frac{1}{2}$ Tbsp (25 mL) chopped herbs

diced tomato for garnish

Preheat oven to 450°F (230°C). Season pork belly with salt and pepper and roast for 45 minutes until golden brown. Cover with foil and reduce heat to 300°F (150°C). Cook 2 hours longer until it provides little resistance to a fork. Cool and cut into six 1$\frac{1}{2}$ oz (43 g) portions. Reheat in a 300°F (150°C) oven for 30 minutes when ready to serve.

For stewed mushrooms and vegetables, melt butter in a medium saucepan over medium-low. Add onion and cook for 1 minute. Add celery, mushrooms and salt. Cover; continue cooking until soft. Combine with demi glace.

For polenta, preheat oven to 300°F (150°C). Sweat off carrots, shallots and garlic in butter. Season with salt and pepper. Add milk and cream. Bring to a boil and whisk in cornmeal. Cover and place in oven for 45 minutes until cornmeal loses all of its graininess. Then fold in cheese and herbs. Check seasoning and adjust if necessary.

To serve, place a spoonful of stewed mushrooms and vegetables in sauce in a soup plate. Pool polenta over top, place reheated pork belly in centre, and top with diced tomato.

Pork bellies are boneless cuts of fatty meat from the underside of a pig. Pork bellies are also cured and smoked to make bacon.

Choucroute

Serves 4

4 garlic cloves, peeled and crushed

3 cloves

1 bay leaf

5 sprigs of thyme

6 juniper berries

15 black peppercorns

1¾ lbs (790 g) sauerkraut

7 oz (200 g) duck fat, divided

1⅓ lbs (600 g) speck (or pancetta), cut into 4 even pieces

1 white onion, sliced thinly

2 cups (500 mL) Riesling wine

1 smoked pork hock

3 cups (750 mL) chicken stock, divided

1¾ lbs (790 g) kassler (smoked pork loin)

4 jaggerwurst sausage (hunter's sausage)

4 small russet potatoes, peeled and cut in half

Dijon mustard to serve

Preheat oven to 325°F (160°C). Make a bouquet garni by tying garlic, cloves, bay leaf, thyme, juniper berries and black peppercorns in cheesecloth. Rinse sauerkraut 2 to 3 times and squeeze out liquid.

Heat half of duck fat in an ovenproof pot over medium. Add speck fat-side down and render fat for 1 to 2 minutes. Add onion and cook until clear. Add wine and reduce by half. Add sauerkraut, bouquet garni, pork hock and 2 cups (500 mL) chicken stock; bring to a simmer. Cook, covered, in preheated oven for 1 hour.

Add kassler; return to oven for another 30 minutes. Sear sausage in remaining duck fat; add to pot. Add potatoes and more stock if needed. Return to oven for another 30 minutes until potatoes are cooked. The speck should be soft to the touch and the rest of the meat cooked to an internal temperature of 160°F (71°C). Remove bouquet garni.

Serve equal portions of all meat with sauerkraut, potatoes and Dijon mustard.

Marinated Rack of Lamb with Honey Pumpkin Seed Crust and Inniskillin Merlot Essence

Serves 4

Honey Mustard Crust

1 Tbsp (15 mL) Canadian mustard

1 Tbsp (15 mL) Canadian honey

2 tsp (10 mL) chopped fresh parsley

Lamb

1 cup (250 mL) olive oil

½ cup (125 mL) dry white wine

1 Tbsp (15 mL) chopped garlic

2 tsp (10 mL) chopped fresh thyme

1 tsp (5 mL) chopped fresh rosemary

1 tsp (5 mL) freshly ground black pepper

2 x 1 lb (500 g) racks of lamb

salt and pepper to taste

vegetable oil for searing

2 Tbsp (30 mL) toasted pumpkin seeds

Parsnip Chips

oil for deep frying

8 oz (225 g) parsnips, trimmed and peeled

salt and pepper to taste

chopped fresh parsley for garnish

Mix together mustard, honey and parsley in small bowl; set aside.

Whisk oil, wine, garlic, thyme, rosemary and pepper together in a glass or stainless steel bowl large enough to hold lamb racks. Marinate lamb racks for 6 to 8 hours in fridge, turning occasionally.

Preheat oven to 380°F (195°C). Remove lamb from marinade. Season with salt. Sear in a hot pan with a little oil to seal. Transfer to baking sheet and roast for about 15 minutes.

Remove from oven, brush with honey mustard mix, then coat with pumpkin seeds. Return to oven for 5 minutes. Remove from oven and let rest for 5 minutes before slicing.

For parsnip chips, heat oil in deep fryer to 350°F (175°C). Thinly slice parsnips in a bias using a knife or a mandoline. Wash parsnip slices and then let stand in ice-cold, salted water for 10 minutes. Drain on a cloth before deep frying until golden brown. Transfer to paper towels to drain; season with salt, pepper and parsley.

(continued on next page)

For sauce, sweat shallots in a hot pan with oil. Add mushrooms, wine, lamb stock, thyme and marmalade. Reduce by two-thirds. Add cranberries and bring sauce back to a rolling boil. Season with salt and pepper. Remove pan from heat and add chilled butter.

To serve, cut racks into double-bone chops and arrange on 4 warm plates. Spoon sauce around meat and place parsnip chips on top.

Sauce

2 oz (57 g) chopped shallots

2 Tbsp (30 mL) olive oil

2 oz (57 g) sliced portobello mushrooms

1 cup (250 mL) Inniskillin merlot wine

2 cups (500 mL) lamb or meat stock

$\frac{1}{4}$ oz (7 g) chopped fresh thyme

2 oz (57 g) lemon marmalade

3 oz (85 g) air-dried cranberries

salt and pepper to taste

3 oz (85 g) butter, chilled

Braised Local Lamb Shanks, Lentil Ragout and Buttered Fava Beans

Serves 4

⅞ cup (200 mL) vegetable oil, divided

4 lamb shanks

salt and pepper to taste

1 onion, diced

1 carrot, peeled and diced

4 garlic cloves

2 cups (500 mL) red wine

8 cups (2 L) chicken stock

2 black cardamom pods

1 cinnamon stick

10 black peppercorns

1 bay leaf

Natural Reduction

⅞ cup (200 mL) rice wine vinegar

3½ oz (100 g) sugar

1 sprig of thyme

Lentil Ragout

7 oz (200 g) beluga lentils

½ white onion, diced

1 shallot, diced finely

3 Tbsp (45 mL) butter

2 oz (57 g) finely diced carrot

1½ Tbsp (25 mL) sherry vinegar

2 tsp (10 mL) honey

salt and pepper to taste

5 leaves parsley, chopped

Drizzle 3 Tbsp (45 mL) oil on lamb shanks and season with salt and pepper. In a large pot on medium-high, sear shanks with remaining oil until golden brown. Sear in batches if the pot is not big enough.

Remove lamb from pot. Sear onion, carrot and garlic until golden brown. Deglaze pot with red wine and reduce until liquid is almost evaporated. Place lamb back in pot and cover with chicken stock. Add cardamom, cinnamon, peppercorns and bay leaf and bring to a simmer for 3 hours. Remove lamb from pot. Strain and reserve braising liquid. Allow to cool, then refrigerate until ready to serve.

For natural reduction, heat vinegar and sugar in a pot over high and reduce by 75%. Add remaining reserved braising liquid and reduce by another 75%. Strain once more through a fine-mesh strainer and reserve finished sauce. Sauce should have a slightly thick consistency.

If sauce is not the right consistency, it can be thickened with a cornstarch slurry (equal parts cold water and cornstarch mixed in a small bowl). Steep thyme in sauce for 5 minutes before straining sauce a final time.

For lentil ragout, place lentils and onion in a small pot and cover with water. Bring to a boil and simmer for about 15 minutes until lentils are tender. Add more water if necessary.

Meanwhile, in a small pan, sweat shallot over low with butter. Add carrot and cook until tender. Add cooked lentils, vinegar and honey. Reduce by half and add 1 Tbsp (15 mL) natural reduction; season with salt and pepper to taste. Just before serving, fold in chopped parsley.

For fava beans, sweat shallot in butter on low until translucent. Add fava beans, chicken stock, salt and pepper. Reduce chicken stock for about 2 minutes until fava beans are glazed.

(continued on next page)

To serve, preheat oven to 350°F (175°C). Place lamb shanks carefully in a shallow pan and season with salt and pepper. Pour ³⁄₄ cup (175 mL) reserved braising liquid over shanks and place in oven for 10 minutes, basting occasionally. Serve immediately.

Place a quarter of lentils in centre of each plate and pat them down to form a circle shape. Top with fava beans; carefully place lamb shank on top. Drizzle 1 tsp (5 mL) natural reduction over lamb. Garnish lamb with a sprig of parsley and enjoy.

Fava Beans

1 shallot, finely diced

2 Tbsp (30 mL) butter

2 cups (500 mL) fava beans, peeled and blanched

3 Tbsp (45 mL) chicken stock

salt and pepper to taste

4 sprigs of parsley for garnish

Natural Venison Meat Loaf with Double-smoked Bacon and Krause Farms Wild Blackberry and Red Wine Sauce

Serves 4

1 lb (500 g) ground venison

¼ lb (113 g) ground pork

2 pinches *each* of kosher salt and black pepper

2 Tbsp (30 mL) finely chopped fresh thyme

¼ cup (60 mL) chopped walnuts

1 Tbsp (15 mL) finely chopped juniper berries

1½ Tbsp (25 mL) vegetable oil, divided

½ cup (125 mL) finely chopped shallots

2 Tbsp (30 mL) brandy

2 Tbsp (30 mL) red wine vinegar

12 to 15 smoked maple bacon slices

Honey Roasted Butternut Squash

1 Tbsp (15 mL) vegetable oil

1 butternut squash, cut into bars

1 tsp (5 mL) brown sugar

2 Tbsp (30 mL) honey

Preheat oven to 350°F (175°C). Mix venison, pork, salt, pepper, thyme, walnuts and juniper berries. Put a little oil in a heated saucepan over medium. Add shallots and cook until translucent. Add brandy and vinegar; reduce slightly. Remove from heat, cool and add to meat mixture.

Line a large loaf pan (or several mini loaf pans) with bacon slices, leaving an overlap so that you can wrap bacon around top of loaf. Fill pan with meat mixture and wrap bacon slices over top. Cook in oven for 25 minutes. Remove from oven and let rest.

For butternut squash, heat a sauté pan over medium; add oil and sauté squash until lightly golden on both sides. Add brown sugar and honey. Mix well. Cook until lightly caramelized (or finish in oven).

(continued on next page)

For sauce, heat a small saucepan on medium. Add remaining oil and shallots; sauté until clear. Add blackberries, wine and honey. Cook slowly over low, reducing to one-quarter. Keep hot for plating.

To serve, slice meat loaf (or leave whole if using mini loaf pans). Place on plates with squash and blackberry wine sauce. Serve with mashed or roasted potatoes if desired.

Blackberry and Red Wine Sauce

1 Tbsp (15 mL) vegetable oil

2 Tbsp (30 mL) finely chopped shallots

2 cups (500 mL) fresh or frozen blackberries

2 cups (500 mL) red wine

2 Tbsp (30 mL) honey

Québec Meat Pie with Game and Mushrooms

Makes 2 pies

1½ cups (375 mL) chopped onion

2 garlic cloves, chopped

1 Tbsp (15 mL) butter

14 oz (400 g) bison (or caribou, wapiti or deer), minced

14 oz (400 g) medium lean pork, minced

2 cups (500 mL) coarsely chopped mushrooms

½ tsp (2 mL) thyme leaves

½ tsp (2 mL) allspice

½ cup (125 mL) oats

2 cups (500 mL) chicken broth

¼ cup (60 mL) chopped parsley

salt and pepper to taste

2 lbs (900 g) pie dough

1 egg whisked with 1 Tbsp (15 mL) milk or water for egg wash

Sauté onion and garlic in butter. Add bison and pork and stir. Let simmer for about 15 minutes. Add mushrooms, thyme, allspice, oats and chicken broth. Mix well and cook slowly for 15 minutes until liquid is absorbed. Add parsley, salt and pepper. Check seasoning and adjust as necessary. Let cool.

Preheat oven to 350°F (175°C). Divide dough into 4 sections. Roll out dough and line two 9 inch (23 cm) pie plates. Put cold meat mixture in pie plates. Brush some egg wash on edges. Cover with same-sized pastry round and seal well. Brush egg wash on top. Make some slits to let steam out during baking. Bake for 40 to 45 minutes until golden brown.

Savoury meat pies are a traditional French-Canadian dish known as tourtière.

Sidney Island Racks of Venison with Saanich Blackberry Glaze

Serves 8

Blackberry Glaze

6 Tbsp (100 mL) red wine

3 Tbsp (45 mL) grainy mustard

1 shallot, minced

1 tsp (5 mL) crushed juniper

rosemary stems

7/8 cup (200 mL) blackberry preserve (homemade or store-bought)

Venison Racks

3 lbs (1.4 kg) venison racks, seasoned generously with salt and pepper and brushed with olive oil

Rosemary Butter-roasted Parsnips

1/2 white onion, cut into medium dice

4 sprigs of fresh rosemary, chopped, divided

1 cup (250 mL) cubed butter, divided

12 small parsnips, trimmed and peeled

salt and pepper to taste

Combine red wine, mustard, shallot, juniper and rosemary and reduce until slightly thickened. Add blackberry preserve, bring to a simmer, then remove from heat and set aside.

For vension racks, preheat oven to 250°F (120°C). Heat a sauté pan on high and sear all sides of venison racks, 1 rack at a time. Brush venison with half of blackberry glaze. Transfer seared racks to ovenproof pan and roast for 15 to 20 minutes until racks reach an internal temperature of 140°F (60°C). Once cooked, brush on remaining glaze and let meat rest for 5 to 10 minutes to allow juices to settle before slicing.

For parsnips, preheat oven to 350°F (175°C). Sauté onion with 2 sprigs rosemary in 1/2 cup (125 mL) butter until rosemary is very aromatic and onions are soft. Pour over parsnips, toss and season. Bake, covered, for 20 minutes until parsnips are soft, then uncover and bake for an additional 10 minutes to caramelize them. When parsnips are soft and golden brown on the edges, add remaining butter and rosemary and toss until melted. Adjust seasonings.

Serve parsnips with sliced venison.

Blackberries are everywhere in summer. This recipe is a great way to enjoy them in a savoury application, long after the season is over. They pair naturally with the mild game flavour of the venison. Rich, buttery parsnips add moisture and richness to the lean meat.

Rossdown Farm Roasted Chicken Breast with Garlic and Thyme Potatoes, Red Onion Marmalade and Pan Jus

Serves 4

1 Tbsp (15 mL) vegetable oil

4 chicken breasts (free-range if possible), skin on

2 pinches *each* of kosher salt and black pepper

1 tsp (5 mL) unsalted butter

Pan Jus

¼ cup (60 mL) white wine

½ cup (125 mL) chicken stock

2 Tbsp (30 mL) cubed, cold butter

Garlic and Thyme Potatoes

1 Tbsp (15 mL) canola oil

8 baby nugget potatoes, sliced into ¼ inch (6 mm) disks

4 garlic cloves, peeled

2 tsp (10 mL) finely chopped fresh thyme

salt and pepper to taste

Preheat oven to 350°F (175°C). Heat sauté pan on high, and add oil. Season chicken with salt and pepper. Place skin-side down in hot oil. Sear for 2 minutes, then flip over and transfer to oven. Cook for 5 to 8 minutes until chicken is fully cooked. Set sauté pan aside. Add butter to top of chicken and let rest.

For pan jus, heat same pan over high. Deglaze with white wine and chicken stock. Reduce for 1 minute and turn heat to low. Add cold butter cubes, and whisk in slowly to thicken sauce.

For potatoes, heat a pan over high and add oil. Add potatoes, garlic and thyme. Cook on high for 1 minute until potatoes are golden in colour. Stir and reduce heat to low. Add a pinch each of salt and pepper and continue to cook until potatoes are tender.

(continued on next page)

For marmalade, heat oil in a saucepan on high. Add onion and sauté for 1 minute. Turn heat to low and add vinegar and sugar. Reduce mixture until caramelized and thick.

To serve, place potatoes on each plate. Slice chicken on an angle and plate on potatoes. Serve with marmalade and pan jus as shown.

Red Onion Marmalade

1 Tbsp (15 mL) vegetable oil

½ red onion, thinly sliced

¼ cup (60 mL) sherry vinegar

3 Tbsp (45 mL) white sugar

Bacon-wrapped Chicken Breast with Creamy Roasted Corn Polenta

Serves 4

16 slices of bacon

4 boneless, skinless chicken breasts

4 sprigs of fresh thyme, leaves chopped

salt and pepper to taste

Creamy Roasted Corn Polenta

3½ oz (100 g) corn niblets, fresh or frozen

3 Tbsp (45 mL) butter, divided

3 oz (85 g) minced shallots

4 cups (1 L) chicken stock

6 oz (175 g) cornmeal

⅞ cup (200 mL) milk

3 oz (85 g) grated Parmesan

3 oz (85 g) cubed butter

fresh herbs or watercress for garnish

Preheat oven to 400°F (200°C). Lay out foil and top each piece with parchment paper, then lay 4 slices of bacon on each. Place each chicken breast on top of bacon on 1 end of parchment paper. Sprinkle chicken with thyme, salt and pepper. Wrap bacon around chicken breast and twist each end of the foil up. Bake chicken for 25 minutes.

Let rest for 10 minutes. Remove foil and parchment paper, and brown chicken breasts in a non-stick pan until bacon is crisp.

For polenta, preheat oven to 400°F (200°C). Toss corn in half of butter. Spread on a baking pan with sides and roast for 10 to 12 minutes.

Sweat shallots in remaining butter. Add chicken stock and bring to a simmer. Slowly add cornmeal, stirring constantly to prevent lumps. Simmer for 10 minutes, then add milk and continue cooking for another 10 minutes. Add corn and Parmesan. Remove from heat; add butter.

To serve, place a spoonful of polenta in middle of 4 bowls and place chicken breast on top. Garnish with fresh herbs or a small bunch of watercress.

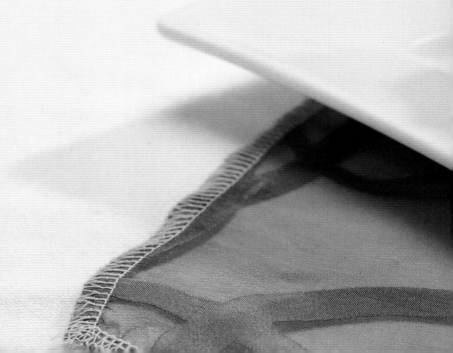

Flamish Chicken in Dark Beer

Serves 8

2 x 4½ lbs (2 kg) chickens, each cut into 8 portions

2 Tbsp (30 mL) all-purpose flour, seasoned with salt and pepper

1 oz (28 g) butter

1 Tbsp (15 mL) canola oil

½ cup (125 mL) Holland or Dutch gin (Genievre)

1 cup (250 mL) diced celery

1 cup (250 mL) peeled and diced carrots

2 shallots, chopped

3 juniper berries, crushed

½ lb (225 g) mushrooms, halved

bouquet garni of 1 parsley stem, 2 bay leaves and 1 sprig of thyme

2 cups (500 mL) dark beer

½ cup (125 mL) crème fraîche

salt and pepper to taste

1 Tbsp (15 mL) chopped fresh flat-leaf parsley for garnish

Dredge chicken pieces in flour; shake well to remove excess. Heat butter and oil in a large pan over high. Add chicken; sauté for 5 minutes on each side to get a nice colour. Add gin and carefully bring edge of pan over flame to flambé, or use a lighter. Be very careful, as there will be at least 1 foot (30 cm) of flame. Remove chicken from pan; keep warm.

Add celery, carrots, shallots and juniper berries to pan; sauté for 5 minutes until vegetables are tender, stirring occasionally. Add mushrooms and bouquet garni to pan. Return chicken to pan. Stir in beer; bring to a simmer. Cover, reduce heat and simmer for 35 to 45 minutes until chicken is cooked.

When done, remove chicken from pan; keep warm. Discard bouquet garni. Place pan over medium; stir in crème fraîche. Cook for 5 minutes. Remove from heat; taste and adjust seasoning with salt and pepper. Pour sauce over chicken and sprinkle with parsley.

A bouquet garni is a collection of flavourful herbs such as parsley, bay leaves and thyme tied together in cheesecloth or just tied together. It is removed once the dish is cooked.

Herb-roasted Polderside Farms Chicken, Roasted Baby Nugget Potatoes with Bacon, Glazed French Beans and Tomato Jam

Serves 4

1 sprig of rosemary

2 sprigs of fresh thyme

10 fresh sage leaves

6 Tbsp (100 mL) vegetable oil

4½ lbs (2 kg) roasting chicken, cleaned and trussed

salt and pepper to taste

Roasted Baby Nugget Potatoes with Bacon

2 bacon slices, cut into ½ inch (12 mm) pieces

8 baby nugget potatoes

salt and pepper to taste

Glazed French Beans

1 shallot, diced

2 Tbsp (30 mL) butter

20 french beans, cleaned and blanched

¼ cup (60 mL) chicken stock

salt and pepper to taste

Preheat oven to 325°F (160°C). Wash rosemary, thyme and sage and place in a blender. Cover with oil and purée for 20 seconds.

Place chicken in a roasting pan and evenly cover with herb oil. Season with salt and pepper and place on middle rack in oven. Cook for 45 minutes until internal temperature reaches 165°F (74°C) on an instant-read thermometer.

Once chicken is cooked, remove from oven and cover loosely with foil for 10 minutes to allow juices to redistribute themselves throughout chicken.

For potatoes, sear bacon until half cooked in a large non-stick ovenproof pan. Remove bacon and add potatoes to pan. Season with salt and pepper and toss potatoes around in bacon fat until evenly covered. Cook potatoes for 5 minutes, tossing occasionally. Return bacon to pan; transfer to oven to finish cooking for about 20 minutes, depending on size of potatoes. Check with a paring knife to ensure potatoes are cooked before serving.

For french beans, sweat shallots in butter over low until translucent. Add beans and chicken stock and season to taste with salt and pepper. Reduce stock for about 2 minutes until beans are glazed.

(continued on next page)

Place all jam ingredients in a pot and simmer until almost dry. Discard cardamom and cinnamon. Transfer jam to blender and blend until smooth. Return jam to pot and reduce to jam consistency.

To serve, remove butcher twine from the trussed bird and place chicken in middle of a serving platter, surrounded by potatoes and beans. Serve jam on side.

Tomato Jam

4 oz (113 g) can chopped tomatoes

½ cup (125 mL) brown sugar

¼ cup (60 mL) rice wine vinegar

2 black cardamom pods

1 stick cinnamon

Makkhani Murhi
(Chicken in Butter Sauce)

Serves 8

Chicken

2 x 3 lb (1.4 kg) chickens, skin removed and cut into 8 pieces each

2 tsp (10 mL) salt

juice from 2 lemons

30 oz (840 mL) plain yogurt

1 Spanish onion, chopped

2 garlic cloves, chopped

2 Tbsp (30 mL) chopped ginger

1 jalapeño pepper, chopped

4 tsp (20 mL) garam masala

Make slits in each piece of chicken. Sprinkle with salt and lemon juice and rub lightly. Refrigerate for 20 minutes.

Preheat oven to 450°F (230°C). Combine yogurt, onion, garlic, ginger, jalapeño and garam masala and blend until smooth. Pass through a strainer into a large bowl. Toss chicken pieces with mixture, making sure that each piece is well coated and that mixture goes into all slits.

Shake off excess marinade from each piece of chicken and place on a roasting pan. Bake for 20 minutes until just cooked.

(continued on next page)

A mixture of as many as 12 different spices, garam masala often includes black pepper, cardamom, cinnamon, cloves, coriander, cumin, dried chilies, fennel, mace and nutmeg. This blend is said to add warmth to both the spirit and the palate, which is fitting, since the Indian word garam literally means "warm."

For butter sauce, mix tomato paste in a large measuring cup with enough water to make 2 cups (500 mL). Add remaining ingredients except butter and mix well.

In a large sauté pan, melt butter, then add tomato mixture and bring to a simmer. Cook over medium, stirring continually, until butter is mixed in. Add tandoori chicken pieces, without residual juices, and coat well. Serve with basmati rice, if desired.

Butter Sauce

½ cup (125 mL) tomato paste or purée

water

2 Tbsp (30 mL) chopped ginger

$1\frac{7}{8}$ cup (450 mL) 10% cream

2 tsp (10 mL) garam masala

2 tsp (10 mL) salt

½ tsp (2 mL) sugar

2 jalapeño peppers, finely chopped

1 tsp (5 mL) chipotle Tabasco sauce

2 Tbsp (30 mL) finely chopped coriander

juice from $1\frac{1}{2}$ lemons

2 tsp (10 mL) cumin

1 cup (250 mL) unsalted butter

Gnocchi with Wild Mushrooms and Duck Confit

Serves 4

Gnocchi

1 x 1 lb (500 g) russet potato

1/2 tsp (2 mL) salt

1/4 tsp (1 mL) freshly ground black pepper

1 egg, beaten

1/4 cup (60 mL) all-purpose flour

Duck Confit

4 duck leg portions with thighs attached, skin on

1 Tbsp (15 mL) plus 1/8 tsp (0.5 mL) kosher salt

1/2 tsp (2 mL) freshly ground black pepper

5 garlic cloves

4 bay leaves

4 sprigs of fresh thyme

1 1/2 tsp (7 mL) black peppercorns

1/2 tsp (2 mL) table salt

4 cups (1 L) olive oil

Pierce potato all over with a fork. Microwave for about 12 minutes until tender, turning once. Cut potato in half and scoop flesh into a large bowl; discard skin. Mash potato well with a fork. Mash in salt and pepper. Mix in 3 Tbsp (45 mL) egg; discard remaining egg. Sift flour over potato mixture and knead until just blended.

Divide dough into 4 equal pieces. Roll each piece into a 1/2 inch (12 mm) diameter rope, about 20 inches (50 cm) long. Cut dough into 1 inch (2.5 cm) pieces. Roll each piece of dough over tines of a fork to form grooves.

Cook gnocchi in a large pot of boiling salted water for about 1 minute until they rise to the surface. Continue cooking for about 4 minutes longer until gnocchi are tender. Remove and cool for later use.

For duck confit, lay duck legs skin-side down in a dish. Sprinkle with 1 Tbsp (15 mL) salt and pepper. Place garlic, bay leaves and thyme on each of 2 leg portions. Lay remaining 2 leg portions, flesh to flesh, on top, and sprinkle with remaining 1/8 tsp (0.5 mL) kosher salt. Cover and refrigerate for 12 hours.

Preheat oven to 200°F (95°C). Remove duck from refrigerator. Remove and reserve garlic, bay leaves, thyme and duck fat. Rinse duck with cool water, rubbing off some salt and pepper. Pat dry with paper towel.

Put reserved garlic, bay leaves, thyme and duck fat in bottom of an enamelled cast-iron pot. Sprinkle evenly with peppercorns and salt. Lay duck on top, skin-side down. Add olive oil. Cover and bake for 12 to 14 hours until meat pulls away from the bone. Allow meat to cool in the fat, then pull meat from the bone into bite-sized pieces.

(continued on next page)

To finish, heat a large, heavy sauté pan and add olive oil and $\frac{1}{8}$ cup (30 mL) butter. Add gnocchi and cook until light brown on all sides. Add shallots and pearl onions and cook over medium for 1 to 2 minutes. Add bacon and continue to cook. Add mushrooms and cook for another 1 to 2 minutes; deglaze with a little red wine. Add demi glace and duck; allow sauce to come together and reduce until it begins to coat everything nicely. Add remaining butter and season to taste. Finish with chervil and Parmesan.

To Finish

2 Tbsp (30 mL) extra-virgin olive oil

$\frac{1}{4}$ cup (60 mL) butter, divided

$1\frac{1}{2}$ Tbsp (25 mL) chopped shallots

20 fresh pearl onions, peeled

4 oz (113 g) double-smoked bacon

9 oz (255 g) mushrooms (mix of chanterelles, blue foot, king oysters and button)

red wine for deglazing pan

$1\frac{2}{3}$ cup (400 mL) demi glace

chopped chervil and micro-grated Parmesan to taste

Buckwheat Honey-roasted Duck with Pumpkin Risotto

Serves 2

2 x 5 oz (140 g) duck breasts

1 cup (250 mL) salt

¼ cup (60 mL) freshly ground black pepper

2 Tbsp (30 mL) minced garlic

1 bunch of thyme

zest from 1 orange

¼ cup (60 mL) buckwheat honey

Pumpkin Risotto

3 Tbsp (45 mL) olive oil

1 shallot, minced

1 cup (250 mL) Arborio rice

¼ cup (60 mL) white wine

3 cups (750 mL) chicken stock

¼ cup (60 mL) cooked and puréed fresh pumpkin

3 Tbsp (45 mL) butter

¼ cup (60 mL) freshly shaved Parmesan cheese

salt and pepper to taste

fresh micro herbs for garnish

Pat duck dry with paper towel. Score fat in a diamond pattern (don't cut into meat). Mix salt, pepper, garlic, thyme and orange zest. Sprinkle some salt mixture on a plate and place duck on top. Cover duck with remaining salt mixture. Let stand for 2 hours.

Preheat oven to 350°F (175°C). Rinse salt mixture off duck; pat dry. Heat a pan over medium and sear duck breast fat-side down. Render fat until golden brown; flip and sear other side. Brush with buckwheat honey and roast in oven, basting with honey every few minutes. Cook until duck reaches an internal temperature of 140°F (60°C). Let rest.

For risotto, heat oil in a medium pan; add shallots and sweat. Add rice and cook for 5 minutes, stirring constantly to coat rice with oil and to toast it, but do not brown. Add wine and reduce until almost dry. Slowly add chicken stock 1 ladle at a time, stirring constantly and reducing stock until almost absorbed every time. Repeat as necessary until rice is cooked.

Add pumpkin and stir in evenly. Finish with butter and Parmesan; season with salt and pepper.

To serve, place risotto on each plate. Slice duck breast and fan on top of risotto. Garnish with fresh micro herbs.

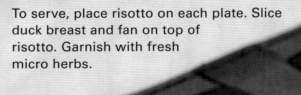

Roasted Duck with Blueberry Sauce

Serves 4

1 whole duck

4 cups (1 L) duck stock or chicken stock

1 Tbsp (15 mL) cinnamon

salt and pepper to taste

2 Tbsp (30 mL) olive oil

1 Tbsp (15 mL) fresh thyme

Blueberry Sauce

2 medium shallots, chopped

½ cup (125 mL) red wine

½ cup (125 mL) red wine vinegar

1 oz (28 g) butter

2 oz (57 g) granulated sugar

1 cup (250 mL) freshly squeezed orange juice

1 cup (250 mL) demi glace

6 Tbsp (100 mL) fresh blueberry purée

50 blueberries for garnish (optional)

Preheat oven to 300°F (150°C). Debone duck and leave legs whole. Brown legs in a hot pan and cover with duck stock; braise in oven for 3 hours. Score fat on breast in a crisscross pattern to allow most of it to render and leave a nice crispy skin. Season duck with cinnamon, salt, pepper, oil and thyme and let stand for 1 hour.

Increase oven temperature to 400°F (200°C). Place duck breast in a hot pan over medium, then place in oven for 7 to 10 minutes. Remove from oven and allow meat to rest for 5 minutes so it reabsorbs its juices.

For sauce, brown shallots in a saucepan. Add wine and reduce by three-quarters, then add vinegar and reduce by three-quarters once more. In a second saucepan, make a light caramel with butter and sugar, then add orange juice and simmer until caramel is dissolved. Combine contents of both pots with demi glace and blueberry purée. Bring to a boil and strain. To serve, place whole berries in sauce for garnish.

Serve duck topped with blueberry sauce.

This dish is beautifully complemented by pommes au gratin, braised red cabbage, glazed carrots, green beans or any other vegetable you love.

Pan-roasted Pheasant Breast with Saskatoon Berry Jus

Serves 2

2 x 6 oz (170 g) pheasant breasts, skin on

salt and pepper to taste

2 Tbsp (30 mL) butter

1 shallot, chopped

2 garlic cloves, chopped

1 sprig of thyme

½ sprig of rosemary

Saskatoon Berry Jus

½ cup (125 mL) red wine

2 cups (500 mL) chicken stock

¼ cup (60 mL) fresh saskatoons

salt and pepper to taste

¼ cup (60 mL) water

2 Tbsp (30 mL) cornstarch

Preheat oven to 350°F (175°C). Season pheasant breasts with salt and pepper. Heat an ovenproof pan and add butter. When butter is melted and starting to brown, add pheasant breasts skin-side down. Flip when golden brown; add shallots, garlic, thyme and rosemary. Transfer to oven and cook, basting with butter every few minutes, until pheasant reaches an internal temperature of 145°F (63°C). Remove pheasant from pan and let rest for 10 minutes.

Drain fat from pan and place pan back on heat. Deglaze with wine and reduce by half, then add chicken stock and reduce by another half. Strain out herbs and shallots, then add saskatoons; season with salt and pepper.

Mix water and cornstarch together and slowly whisk into simmering sauce until lightly thickened. Taste and adjust seasoning.

Slice duck breasts on an angle and place on plates. Pour saskatoon berry jus over and serve.

Maple Vanilla-cured Wild BC Sockeye Salmon with Green Pea Purée and Krause Farms Blueberry and Bourbon Butter

Serves 4

Maple Vanilla Cure

1 cup (250 mL) coarse pickling salt

1 tsp (5 mL) vanilla extract

½ cup (125 mL) brown sugar

zest and juice from 1 lemon

¼ cup (60 mL) maple syrup

Salmon

4 x 5 oz (140 g) salmon fillets

2 pinches *each* of kosher salt and black pepper

2 Tbsp (30 mL) canola oil, divided

8 tsp (40 mL) soft unsalted butter, divided

1 shallot, minced

1 oz (30 mL) bourbon whiskey

1 cup (250 mL) blueberries

1 bunch of chives, chopped

Preheat oven to 350°F (175°C). Mix cure ingredients in a bowl.

Put salmon fillets in bowl of cure; make sure that cure covers them all. Cover and refrigerate for 10 minutes.

Remove salmon from bowl, rinse with cold water and pat dry. Season with salt and pepper. Preheat an ovenproof pan and heat 1 Tbsp (15 mL) oil. Sear salmon on 1 side only. Transfer pan to oven for 3 to 4 minutes, depending on thickness of salmon. Smear salmon with 4 tsp (20 mL) butter when it comes out of the oven.

Heat remaining oil in a small saucepan over medium and add shallots; sauté until clear. Remove pan from heat and add bourbon. Tilt pan on open gas flame to ignite bourbon, or use a lighter. Be very careful, as there will be at least 1 foot (30 cm) of flame.

Add blueberries and reduce for 3 to 5 minutes until they are soft. Take off heat and slowly whisk in remaining butter and chives.

(continued on next page)

Cook peas in boiling water for 30 seconds. Transfer to blender and add stock and pinch of salt and pepper. Purée until smooth.

To serve, garnish salmon with mustard greens and radish. Serve with green pea purée.

Green Pea Purée

1 cup (250 mL) frozen green peas

¼ cup (60 mL) chicken stock

salt and pepper to taste

Garnish

4 oz (113 g) mustard greens or arugula

2 oz (57 g) sliced radish

BC Spot Prawn and Wild Salmon Cakes with Firecracker Rice and Kaffir Lemongrass Sauce

Serves 4

$1^3/_4$ oz (50 g) fresh white bread, crust removed

$1^1/_3$ lbs (600 g) spot prawns, shelled and coarsely chopped

9 oz (255 g) wild salmon fillet, fat removed and coarsely chopped

2 oz (57 g) mayonnaise

2 oz (57 g) cream cheese, softened

3 green onions, minced

juice from $^1/_2$ lemon

salt and pepper to taste

2 oz (57 g) panko

vegetable oil

Firecracker Rice

1 oz (28 g) butter

$1^2/_3$ cups (400 mL) basmati rice, rinsed

$^1/_4$ Tbsp (3 mL) vanilla, or $^1/_2$ vanilla bean, split

2 Tbsp (30 mL) sambal oelek

$2^1/_2$ cups (625 mL) water

Place fresh bread slices in food processor and pulse into soft bread crumbs (not too fine). Mix spot prawns, salmon, mayonnaise, cream cheese, green onions, lemon juice, salt and pepper in a medium bowl. Add bread crumbs, mix gently and season.

Spread half of panko on a small tray and place $^1/_4$ of fish cake mixture into a round food ring or form into patty shape. Pat fish cakes into panko. Sprinkle remaining panko on top of fish cakes. Preheat a pan with a splash of vegetable oil to cover bottom; cook cakes until light golden and internal temperature reaches 122°F (50°C). Remove to tea towel and keep warm.

For rice, melt butter in a pot with a tight-fitting lid; add rice, vanilla, sambal oelek and water. Bring to a quick boil and reduce. Simmer, covered, for 8 to 10 minutes. Remove from heat and let rest for 5 minutes before serving.

(continued on next page)

For sauce, cook garlic, ginger and green onions in oil until soft. Add chicken stock, fish paste, lemongrass, kaffir and turmeric. Simmer for 5 minutes and then add coconut milk, cilantro, lime juice and brown sugar. Simmer to the consistency of a thin sauce. Strain and reserve.

To serve, place moulded rice in centre of a large bowl and pour sauce and some vegetables around rice. Then place fish cake on top or beside rice.

Serve this dish with some lightly sautéed vegetables and a garnish of julienned carrot and baby pea shoots. Baby pea shoots are found in the produce section of grocery stores with the fresh herbs and sprouts.

Kaffir Lemongrass Sauce

1 garlic clove, chopped

2 Tbsp (30 mL) chopped ginger

2 green onions, chopped

1 tsp (5 mL) sesame oil

6 Tbsp (100 mL) chicken stock

½ tsp (2 mL) fish paste

1 stalk of lemongrass

3 kaffir lime leaves

½ tsp (2 mL) turmeric

1⅔ cups (400 mL) coconut milk

2 tsp (10 mL) chopped cilantro

juice from ½ lime

1 Tbsp (15 mL) brown sugar

Thyme Butter-baked Sockeye Salmon with Buttered Spaetzle, Sautéed Pearl Onions and Chanterelle Mushrooms

Serves 8

3 oz (85 g) cold butter, cubed and divided

4 sprigs of thyme

1 shallot, minced

zest from 1 lemon

salt and pepper to taste

8 x ⅓ lb (150 g) skinless sockeye fillets

Buttered Spaetzle

3¼ cups (800 mL) all-purpose flour

1⅔ cups (400 mL) milk

1⅔ cups (400 mL) whole egg

2 tsp (10 mL) ground caraway seeds

salt and pepper to taste

Onions and Mushrooms

40 pearl onions, trimmed and peeled

1 cup (250 mL) chanterelle mushrooms, trimmed and gently rinsed

3 Tbsp (45 mL) butter

Combine half of butter with thyme, shallots, zest, salt and pepper in a sauté pan and bring to a simmer. Remove from heat and stir in remaining butter until emulsified. Allow to cool to room temperature, then pour over salmon; refrigerate overnight.

Preheat oven to 200°F (95°C). Bake salmon for 12 to 15 minutes, depending on thickness of fillets. Salmon is cooked when it is slightly firm.

Combine spaetzle ingredients in a stand mixer and mix, using paddle attachment, for 5 to 7 minutes on medium until dough is smooth and somewhat elastic. Allow to rest for 1 hour.

To cook spaetzle, transfer dough to a piping bag fitted with a ⅓ inch (1 cm) tip. Bring a large stock pot of salted water to a simmer. Drop ¾ inch (2 cm) long pieces of dough into the water. Allow spaetzle to float to the surface. Remove and cool on a baking sheet.

Sauté onions and mushrooms in butter over medium-high for 5 to 7 minutes. Once onions are tender, add cooked spaetzle and toss. Serve immediately with salmon.

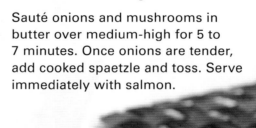

Sockeye salmon and chanterelles are freshest and most abundant in late summer. Baking the salmon at a low temperature helps the fish to retain all its natural flavour and moisture. Sautéing the spaetzle with the chanterelles helps the spaetzle to absorb all the flavour and aroma the mushrooms have to offer.

Smoked Salmon with Phyllo Crust

Serves 6

1 lb (500 g) salmon fillet, all bones carefully removed

3 Tbsp (45 mL) coarse salt

4½ oz (125 g) brown sugar

aromatics such as shallots, dill or lemon zest to taste

Honey Glaze

1 shallot, finely diced

¼ oz (7 g) butter

½ cup (125 mL) white wine

3½ oz (100 g) honey

Phyllo Crusts

4 phyllo sheets

3 Tbsp (45 g) butter, melted

6 Tbsp (100 mL) *each* parsley and dill, roughly chopped

Garnish

garnish of dressed pea shoots, arugula or watercress

capers, honey mustard and crème fraîche

Lay salmon on a flat pan and sprinkle with salt, brown sugar and aromatics, and refrigerate for 24 hours. Flip salmon and refrigerate for an additional 24 hours. Repeat as desired.

Once desired cure of salmon is reached (usually 3 days, depending on the thickness of the fillet), remove salmon from cure, rinse and pat dry. Place on a wire rack above smoke chips in barbecue and smoke for 30 minutes, glazing every 10 minutes with honey glaze.

For honey glaze, sauté shallots in butter until soft, then add wine and reduce by half. Combine with honey and cook until syrupy. Spread glaze over salmon as it smokes.

For phyllo crusts, preheat oven to 400°F (200°C). Lay 1 sheet of phyllo on a cutting board and brush with melted butter and sprinkle with herbs; repeat until all 4 layers are on. Cut into 6 equal squares and bake for about 4 to 5 minutes until golden.

To serve, place 1 phyllo crust flat on each plate, dress some nice salad of pea shoots, arugula or watercress, and place on top. Thinly slice salmon and lay over top. Sprinkle with capers, drizzle with honey mustard and finish with a couple small dollops of crème fraîche on each plate.

Grilled Haida Gwaii Halibut with Citrus Ricotta Gnocchi and Cherry Tomato Caper Ragout

Serves 8

Citrus Ricotta Gnocchi

9 oz (255 g) all-purpose flour

9 oz (225 g) ricotta

zest of 1 orange

1/3 oz (10 g) ground fennel seeds

salt and pepper to taste

Cherry Tomato and Caper Ragout

40 cherry tomatoes, cut in half

3 Tbsp (45 mL) drained capers

2 garlic cloves, thinly sliced

3½ oz (100 g) julienned red onion

salt and pepper to taste

3 Tbsp (45 mL) olive oil

Grilled Halibut

canola oil for wiping grill

8 x 1/3 lb (150 g) halibut fillets

salt and pepper to taste

olive oil

juice from 1 lemon

Combine flour, ricotta, orange zest and fennel seeds in a bowl until dough forms. Transfer to a work surface and knead for 3 to 5 minutes, then allow to rest for 1 hour.

Roll dough into logs about the thickness of your thumb, then cut into 3/4 inch (2 cm) long pieces. Place gnocchi in lightly salted boiling water. Allow gnocchi to float for 2 to 3 minutes before retrieving with a slotted spoon, then cool on an oiled baking tray.

Sauté tomatoes, capers, garlic, red onion, salt and pepper in oil over medium-high until tomatoes soften. Remove from heat and reserve in fridge.

For halibut, preheat grill to medium-high and clean thoroughly. Spray or wipe grill with a small amount of canola oil. Sprinkle halibut with salt and pepper on both sides and place on grill 2 to 3 inches (5 to 7.5 cm) apart. Give fish a 1/4 turn after 3 minutes, then flip over after an additional 3 minutes. Once flipped, reduce heat to medium and cook for 3 to 5 minutes to finish the halibut.

Meanwhile, sauté cooked gnocchi in a small amount of olive oil until golden brown. Add ragout to gnocchi and toss until ragout is warm.

Once halibut is cooked, remove from grill and place on top of ragout and gnocchi. Finish with generous amounts of olive oil and lemon juice.

Halibut is in season all summer. With its mild flavour and flaky texture, it is perfect for a light, fresh summer dinner. The gnocchi and ragout can both be done up to 24 hours in advance, which will ease preparation and allows time to ensure that the halibut is cooked perfectly on the grill.

Seared Halibut with Arugula, Roasted Beets and Horseradish Mayonnaise

Serves 4

4 x 5 to 6 oz (140 to 170 g) boneless halibut fillets

zest of 1 lemon

1 Tbsp (15 mL) thyme leaves

2 Tbsp (30 mL) coarsely chopped flat-leaf parsley

1 Tbsp (15 mL) grated fresh horseradish

½ cup (125 mL) mayonnaise

salt and pepper to taste

2 Tbsp (30 mL) extra-virgin olive oil, divided, plus extra for drizzling

4 roasted beets, thinly sliced

4 oz (113 g) cleaned arugula

Season halibut with lemon zest, thyme and parsley. Let stand at room temperature for 15 minutes. Meanwhile, mix horseradish and mayonnaise; season with salt and pepper.

Heat a large sauté pan over high for 2 minutes. Season halibut on both sides with salt and pepper. Add 1 Tbsp (15 mL) olive oil to pan. Carefully lay halibut in pan and cook for 3 to 4 minutes until lightly browned. Flip fish, reduce heat to medium-low and cook for a few more minutes until almost cooked through. Be careful not to overcook fish.

Meanwhile, in another hot pan, heat 1 Tbsp (15 mL) olive oil and add beets. Sauté beets until warm and then add arugula. Season with salt and pepper. When arugula is wilted, remove pan from heat.

To serve, place beets and wilted arugula in the centre of 4 warm plates. Place seared halibut on top and drizzle some olive oil over fish. Spoon horseradish mayonnaise in a dollop beside fish or serve on side as a condiment.

Seared Tuna with Nova Scotia Hodge Podge

Serves 4

4½ oz (125 g) tuna steak

1 tsp (5 mL) kosher salt

¼ tsp (1 mL) cayenne pepper

½ tsp (2 mL) butter

2 Tbsp (30 mL) olive oil

1 tsp (5 mL) whole peppercorns

Nova Scotia Hodge Podge

2 cups (500 mL) cubed new potatoes

1 cup (250 mL) fresh green beans, trimmed and snapped

1 cup (250 mL) fresh wax beans, trimmed and snapped

4 bacon slices, diced

½ cup (125 mL) heavy cream

1 cup (250 mL) corn, freshly shucked or frozen

1 cup (250 mL) fresh peas

salt and pepper to taste

¼ cup (60 mL) green onions, sliced

Season tuna steaks with salt and cayenne pepper. Melt butter with olive oil in a skillet over medium-high. Cook peppercorns in mixture for about 5 minutes until they soften and pop. Gently place seasoned tuna in skillet and cook for about 1½ minutes per side for rare or until desired doneness.

In a large pot, boil potatoes in lightly salted water until almost cooked. Add green beans and wax beans to potatoes for the last 5 minutes. Remove potatoes and beans from water and set aside.

In a sauté pan, cook bacon until crisp. In the same pan, add cream, corn, peas, boiled potatoes and beans. Cover and cook for 10 minutes over medium. Season with salt and pepper.

To serve, place hodge podge on a warm plate and garnish with green onions. Slice tuna steak into 4 pieces and lay on top of hodge podge.

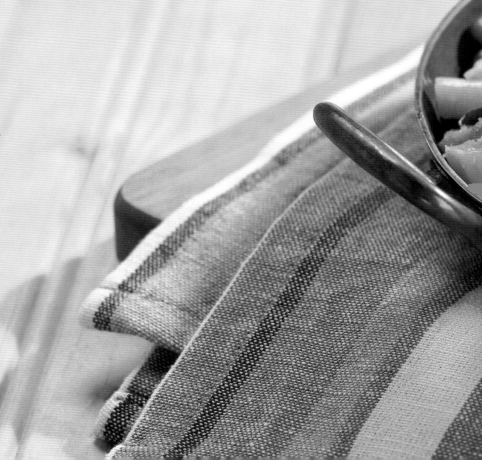

Serve this dish with some lightly sautéed vegetables and a garnish of julienned carrot and baby pea shoots. Baby pea shoots are found in the produce section of grocery stores with the fresh herbs and sprouts.

Serrano Ham-wrapped Cod Loin with Split Pea Purée

Serves 4

4 large slices Serrano ham

4 x 6 oz (170 g) centre loin cod fillets

4 Tbsp (60 mL) olive oil

Split Pea Purée

1 cup (250 mL) split peas

3 cups (750 mL) water

1 shallot, diced

1 garlic clove, minced

1 small bunch of chives, chopped

2 Tbsp (30 mL) butter

salt and pepper to taste

Preheat oven to 350°F (175°C). Wrap ham tightly around cod loins and brush with olive oil. Bake for about 10 minutes until cod is cooked.

Rinse split peas. Add water, shallots, garlic and peas to pot and bring to boil. Reduce heat to a simmer and cook until water is mostly absorbed and peas are tender. Add extra water if peas are still hard. Once cooked, combine with chives and butter and mix thoroughly. Purée, adding water as needed. Season with salt and pepper.

To serve, dollop a serving of split pea purée on each of 4 plates; top with cod.

Serrano ham is one of Spain's most famous foods. It is a bit drier than prosciutto ham.

Lobster and Chanterelle Risotto

Serves 6

4 cups (1 L) fish stock or water

1 Tbsp (15 mL) olive oil

1 shallot, finely diced

1 garlic clove, finely diced

14 oz (400 g) Arborio rice

½ cup (125 mL) chardonnay

9 oz (255 g) sliced chanterelle mushrooms

2¼ lbs (1 kg) uncooked lobster meat

2½ oz (70 g) butter

⅓ cup (75 mL) chopped dill

salt and pepper to taste

Warm fish stock or water. In a separate pan, heat olive oil. Add shallots and garlic, and sweat vegetables. Add rice, and stirring continuously, begin to add warm stock to rice mixture 1 ladle at a time, stirring until it is absorbed. Then, still stirring, add next ladle full of stock. Continue in this manner until half of liquid is used. Add chardonnay and continue to spoon in 1 ladle of liquid at a time. Just before all liquid is absorbed, add chanterelle mushrooms and lobster. Cook for about 5 minutes and then test rice for doneness.

Once rice is cooked, stir in butter and dill. Season with salt and pepper and serve.

Arborio rice is an Italian variety of short-grain rice used for making risotto. Kernels of arborio rice are shorter and fatter than other types of short-grain rice and have a very high starch content. The starch helps to give risotto its traditionally creamy texture.

Sweet Pea and Lobster Lasagna

Serves 10

olive oil for brushing dish

1 lb (500 g) uncooked lobster meat

1½ cups (375 mL) whipping cream

¼ cup (60 mL) packed, chopped fresh basil leaves

2 cups (500 mL) cottage cheese, divided

1 lb (500 g) bag frozen peas, thawed

¾ cup (175 mL) grated Parmesan cheese

2 large eggs

1 tsp (5 mL) sea salt

12 no-boil lasagna noodles

4 cups (1 L) grated mozzarella cheese, divided

Preheat oven to 400°F (200°C). Brush a 13 x 9 x 2 inch (33 x 23 x 5 cm) glass baking dish with olive oil. Mix lobster meat, cream, basil, 1¼ cups (300 mL) cottage cheese, peas, Parmesan, eggs and salt in a medium bowl. Spread remaining cottage cheese over bottom of prepared baking dish.

Arrange 4 noodles in a single layer over cottage cheese, breaking noodles as needed to cover. Spread ¼ of lobster mixture over noodles. Sprinkle ¼ cup (60 mL) mozzarella cheese over first layer. Repeat 3 more times with 4 noodles, lobster mixture and ¼ cup (60 mL) mozzarella cheese each time.

Top with remaining mozzarella cheese. Cover with foil, sealing edges. Bake for 30 minutes with foil on, and then remove foil and bake for an additional 25 minutes. Let stand for 15 minutes before serving.

Pan-seared Scallops and Ragout of Summer Vegetables in a Phyllo Pastry Frying Pan with Minted Orange Sauce

Serves 4

Phyllo Pastry Frying Pans

8 sheets phyllo pastry, plus 2 sheets cut in half horizontally

⅓ lb (150 g) unsalted butter, melted and clarified

1 tsp (5 mL) salted butter

Minted Orange Sauce

½ cup (125 mL) fish stock

juice from 3 oranges and ½ lemon

1 Tbsp (15 mL) champagne vinegar, white wine vinegar or apple cider vinegar

2 bay leaves

2 Tbsp (30 mL) chopped mint stalks

1 cup (250 mL) whipping cream

1 oz (28 g) cold unsalted butter

salt and pepper to taste

Preheat oven to 325°F (160°C). To make pastry frying pans, brush 1 whole pastry sheet with butter and fold in half. Place in a small cast iron frying pan; mould to the shape of the pan and trim off excess. Butter a half sheet, roll it up to make a handle and lay it partly in the pan but with 8 cm (3 inches) extending up the real pan handle. To secure handle, cover pan area with another folded sheet. Trim it to shape and prick all over with a fork. Brush again with butter. Bake for about 12 minutes until crisp and brown.

Repeat to make 3 more pastry frying pans.

In a saucepan, mix fish stock, fruit juices, vinegar, bay leaves and mint stalks. Bring to a boil, lower heat and reduce by two-thirds. Strain, return to pan and add cream. Simmer for 5 minutes. Whisk in butter in small pieces; do not let it simmer. Season with salt and pepper and set aside.

(continued on next page)

Quickly blanch asparagus, yellow pepper and tomatoes in boiling salted water. Strain, add butter and season. Keep warm.

Season scallops with salt and pepper and sear in very hot pan. Serve scallops in phyllo frying pans with vegetables and minted orange sauce.

Summer Vegetables

asparagus spears

1 yellow pepper, thinly sliced

2 tomatoes, peeled, seeded and diced

Scallops

12 large fresh scallops, patted dry

salt and pepper to taste

Soba Noodles with Asparagus, Digby Scallops and Sweet Miso Sauce

Serves 4

Miso Sauce

3 Tbsp (45 mL) sugar

¼ cup (60 mL) sake

3 Tbsp (45 mL) mirin

2 Tbsp (30 mL) rice vinegar

⅓ cup (75 mL) white miso

1 Tbsp (15 mL) finely grated ginger

1 Tbsp (15 mL) vegetable oil

Scallops and Asparagus

1 Tbsp (15 mL) vegetable oil

16 x 10/20 scallops (see Tip), patted very dry and side mussel removed

kosher salt and pepper to taste

½ cup (125 mL) water

36 medium asparagus tips

Soba Noodles

10 oz (285 g) dried soba noodles

2 Tbsp (30 mL) pine nuts, lightly toasted and coarsely chopped

In a pot, whisk together sugar, sake, mirin and rice vinegar until sugar is completely dissolved. Add miso, ginger and oil; whisk until well combined. Keep warm over low until ready to plate.

For scallops, heat oil in a large sauté pan until very hot. Season scallops with salt and pepper on both sides. Place in hot pan, making sure to sear flat side of scallop. Cook on 1 side for about 90 seconds and turn the scallop over to the other flat side and cook for another 90 seconds. If you like scallops well done, leave in the pan a bit longer.

Transfer cooked scallops to a plate to rest for a minute. Leave pan on burner and add water; add asparagus and cover pan. Cook for 60 seconds until just cooked.

Just before you are ready to plate, bring a large pot of water to a boil over high. Cook noodles for about 3 minutes or until they're done to your liking. Drain well and divide among 4 warm plates. Divide scallops and asparagus among plates, and spoon some warm miso sauce over each. Garnish with toasted pine nuts.

Tip

"10/20" refers to the size of the scallops; there are 10 to 20 scallops per pound.

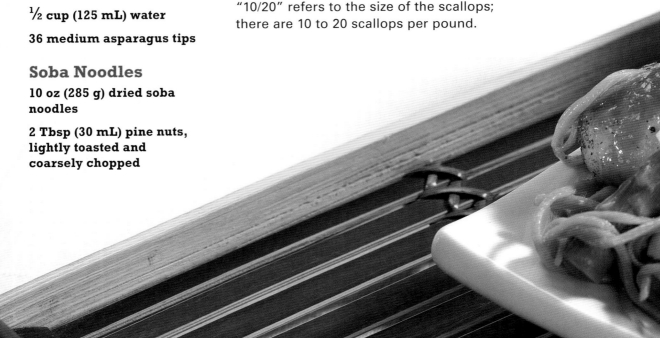

 *Also known as bean paste, miso is an important ingredient in Japanese cuisine. Miso is made from fermented soybeans. The consistency of miso is usually similar to peanut butter, and it is available in a variety of flavours and colours. Generally, lighter colours of miso are good for more delicately flavoured dishes, while darker colours work well with bolder flavours.*

Dover Sole "Meuniere"-style with Capers

Serves 4

4 x ⅓ lb (150 g) Dover sole fillets

½ cup (125 mL) all-purpose flour, seasoned with sea salt and black pepper

¼ cup (60 mL) butter

Sauce

¼ cup (60 mL) unsalted butter

1 Tbsp (15 mL) chopped parsley

1 Tbsp (15 mL) fresh lemon juice

1 Tbsp (15 mL) small capers

lemon wedges for garnish

Rinse fish; pat dry with paper towels. Place seasoned flour in a dish. Dredge fish with flour; shake off excess. Place on platter.

Heat butter in a large skillet over medium-high until butter approaches a chestnut colour. Add fish and cook for about 2 minutes until golden on bottom. Carefully flip fish and cook for about 2 minutes until golden on bottom. Remove fish and keep warm. Pour off drippings from skillet and wipe it clean.

For sauce, place same skillet over medium-high. Add butter and cook for 1 or 2 minutes until golden. Remove from heat; stir in parsley, lemon juice (sauce may sputter) and capers. Spoon sauce on fillets. Serve with lemon wedges.

Hazelnut-crusted Chilliwack Trout with Sweet Pea Risotto and Pea Froth

Serves 4

¼ cup (60 mL) vegetable oil, divided

1 trout, skin on, deboned and portioned into 4 fillets

kosher salt and pepper to taste

⅓ oz (10 g) butter

1 Tbsp (15 mL) balsamic vinegar

juice from ½ lemon

3 oz (85 g) skin-free hazelnuts, toasted and chopped

Sweet Pea Risotto

1 shallot, thinly sliced

3 Tbsp (45 mL) vegetable oil

7 oz (200 g) Arborio rice

6 Tbsp (100 mL) white wine

4 cups (1 L) vegetable stock

3 Tbsp (45 mL) butter

1 oz (28 g) grated Parmesan cheese

3½ oz (100 g) sweet English peas, blanched

salt and pepper to taste

Heat 3 Tbsp (45 mL) oil in a non-stick pan over medium-high. Drizzle remaining oil on fish and season with salt and pepper. Sear fish skin-side down for 1 minute. Flip trout carefully using a fish spatula and sear for 2 minutes. Peel skin off of trout. Place butter in pan and continue to cook for 2 minutes. Add balsamic vinegar and cook for 20 seconds, allowing vinegar to reduce quickly.

Flip trout again; season with lemon juice and sprinkle with hazelnuts. Fish is cooked when internal temperature reaches 125°F (52°C) and fish is firm to the touch.

Sweat shallots with oil in a small pot over medium. Cook until translucent. Add rice and sauté for 2 minutes, stirring occasionally. Deglaze with wine and allow to reduce by 90%. Slowly add a ½ cup (125 mL) ladle of vegetable stock, stirring occasionally. Allow stock to reduce before adding another ladle of stock. Continue adding stock in this manner until rice is 90% cooked and all stock has been used.

Add butter, Parmesan and peas, and season with salt and pepper. Add more vegetable stock if risotto is slightly thick.

(continued on next page)

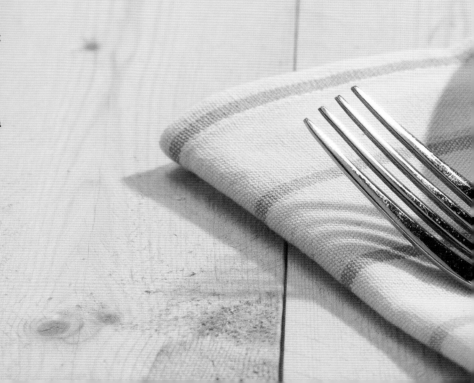

For pea froth, sweat shallots with butter in a small pot over low until translucent. Add wine and allow to reduce by 90%. Add milk and bring to a simmer for 5 minutes. Place peas and liquid in a non-ferrous container (glass or plastic are fine). Carefully blend with a hand blender. Use caution when blending hot liquids. Keep warm and set aside.

To serve, aerate pea liquid with a hand blender, creating a froth. Place a portion of risotto on each plate, top with fish and garnish with pea froth.

Pea Froth

2 shallots, thinly sliced

3 Tbsp (45 mL) butter

¼ cup (60 mL) white wine

2 cups (500 mL) skim milk

3½ oz (100 g) sweet English peas, blanched

Seared Walleye on Creamed Fennel with Tomato Confit

Serves 4

4 x 6 oz (170 g) boneless walleye fillets, skin on and scaled

zest from 1 lemon

2 shallots, diced

2 Tbsp (30 mL) chopped fresh dill

2 oz (57 g) butter

½ onion, diced

1 fennel bulb, diced

⅔ cup (150 mL) white wine

⅔ cup (150 mL) fish stock

⅔ cup (150 mL) heavy cream

salt and pepper to taste

4 cocktail tomatoes

olive oil to cover tomatoes

Rub walleye fillets with lemon zest, shallots and dill. Wrap tightly in plastic wrap and refrigerate for 6 hours.

Place butter in a small pot over medium and sauté onion and fennel for 3 to 5 minutes. Add wine and fish stock and simmer, covered, until fennel is soft and liquid is reduced by half. Add cream and simmer again, uncovered, until three-quarters of liquid is reduced. Carefully purée fennel mixture and season with salt and pepper. Use caution when blending hot liquids. Set aside.

Preheat oven to 300°F (150°C). Place tomatoes in cups of a muffin tin. Cover with olive oil and bake for 15 minutes. Remove from oven. Increase oven temperature to 375°F (190°C).

Wipe lemon zest and dill off salmon and season salmon with salt and pepper. In a hot pan, sear salmon skin-side down until crispy. Flip over and put pan in oven for about 4 minutes until just cooked. Let salmon rest for 3 minutes.

To serve, place creamed fennel on plates. Place salmon on fennel. Top salmon with tomatoes.

Poached Pickerel with a Ragout of Clams, Mussels and Spot Prawns

Serves 4

4 shallots, finely chopped, divided

2 tsp (10 mL) butter, divided

10 mussels

4 cups (1 L) white wine, divided

10 clams

1 cup (250 mL) chicken stock

salt and white pepper to taste

4 x 4 oz (113 g) pickerel fillets

$1\frac{1}{2}$ oz (43 g) cured chorizo

$2\frac{1}{2}$ Tbsp (37 mL) extra-virgin olive oil, plus more for drizzling

1 shallot, cut into thin rings

6 fingerling potatoes, cut into quarters

8 pearl onions, cut in half

4 carrot ribbons (use yellow and orange baby carrots)

2 baby zucchini, cut into coins

4 baby fennel bulbs, thinly sliced

$\frac{7}{8}$ cup (200 mL) spicy clamato juice

8 spot prawns, peeled and deveined

1 tsp (5 mL) chopped basil

sea salt to taste

In a large saucepan, sauté half of shallots in 1 tsp (5 mL) butter over medium until translucent. Add mussels and 2 cups (500 mL) wine. Cover and cook until mussels just open. In a separate saucepan, sauté remaining butter and remaining shallots. Add clams and remaining wine. Cover and cook until clams just open. Discard any mussels and clams that do not open.

Transfer mussels and clams to a bowl. Strain both poaching liquids together in a pan and reduce by half. Add chicken stock and bring to a quick simmer. Season with salt and pepper. Add pickerel and poach for 3 to 4 minutes.

In a large saucepan over medium, render chorizo with oil for 1 to 2 minutes. Add shallot rings, potatoes and pearl onions; sauté for 2 minutes. Add carrot, zucchini and fennel; cook for 1 to 2 minutes. Season with salt and pepper.

Add clamato juice and poaching liquid from mussels and clams; bring to simmer. Add spot prawns, clams and mussels; cook just long enough to cook prawns and warm clams and mussels through again. Finish with a little extra-virgin olive oil and fresh basil.

Divide vegetables and seafood among 4 bowls. Sit pickerel fillets on top. Sprinkle with a little sea salt, and add broth.

Alsatian Onion Tart

Makes 2 x 9 inch (23 cm) deep-dish tarts, or 4 to 6 servings

2 pie shells (use purchased or make 1 lb [500 g] pie dough)

3½ oz (100 g) well-smoked, unsliced bacon, diced (lardons)

3 Tbsp (45 mL) butter

2 cups (500 mL) chopped onions

2½ oz (70 g) flour

1½ cups (375 mL) whole milk

1 cup (250 mL) heavy cream

4 eggs, lightly beaten

1 Tbsp (15 mL) chopped parsley

salt, pepper and grated nutmeg to taste

Preheat oven to 350°F (175°C). If making pie dough from scratch, roll out pie shells. Place shells in pie plates. Prick bottom and sides of pie shells with a fork and precook for 10 to 12 minutes until lightly browned. Let cool.

In a saucepan, sauté lardons until lightly brown. Transfer to paper towels to drain, but leave fat in pan. Add butter to pan along with onions; cook over medium until soft and light golden brown. Remove pan from heat and let cool.

In a bowl, mix onions, flour, milk and cream. Add eggs and parsley. Season with salt, pepper and nutmeg. Pour into cooked and cooled pie shells; add diced bacon on top. Place pie plates on a baking sheet and cook for 50 to 60 minutes.

Serve hot with a corn salad (mâche) for an excellent lunch. The tarts can be reheated easily if there are leftovers.

Brioche

Makes 7 brioches

1½ oz (45 mL) water

3½ oz (100 g) whole egg

7 oz (200 g) bread flour

¼ oz (8 g) instant yeast

1 oz (28 g) sugar

¼ oz (7 g) salt

3½ oz (100 g) cold butter, cut into small pieces

melted butter and granulated sugar for topping

Put water and egg together in a mixer with paddle attachment. Add flour, yeast, sugar and salt. Mix on low for 2½ minutes. Increase speed to medium and mix for 4 minutes. Add butter in 4 increments, ensuring dough is well mixed after each addition. Place dough on a pan and cover lightly with plastic wrap. Allow to rest in fridge for at least 6 hours or overnight.

Divide into 7 equal pieces and roll tightly into balls. Allow balls to proof for 3½ to 4 hours until about 4 times the size or until finger indentation in dough does not bounce back for about 5 seconds.

Preheat oven to 325°F (160°C) and bake for 15 to 19 minutes until buns are golden and centre is hollow.

Brush with melted butter and roll in granulated sugar after baking.

Brioche is a type of flaky, rich French bread. It is "enriched," meaning that it has a higher butter content than other breads.

Fairwinds Goat Cheese Soufflé

Serves 4 to 6

3 Tbsp (45 mL) butter, divided

1½ oz (43 g) flour

½ cup (125 mL) milk

salt and pepper to taste

4½ oz (125 g) fresh goat cheese

2 egg yolks

¼ cup (60 mL) egg whites (about 2 egg whites)

1½ oz (43 g) walnuts, finely chopped

Preheat oven to 400°F (200°C). Place 2 Tbsp (30 mL) butter in a small saucepan and make a roux with flour. Add milk, bring to a boil and season to taste with salt and pepper. Place mixture in a large bowl and cool by whisking vigorously.

Cream goat cheese. Add egg yolks and fold into soufflé base.

In a separate bowl, whip egg whites to stiff peaks. Using a spatula, gently fold in egg whites to mixture.

Brush a soufflé dish with remaining butter and line dish with chopped walnuts. Spoon in soufflé batter. Place dish in a high-sided pan partly filled with water and bake for 30 minutes until golden brown.

Remove soufflé dish from oven and serve.

White Chocolate Raspberry Scones

Makes 16 scones

22 oz (620 g) all-purpose flour

3¾ oz (107 g) granulated sugar

1¼ oz (37 g) baking powder

⅓ oz (10 g) salt

5 oz (140 g) cubed, cold butter

3 eggs

1 cup (250 mL) heavy cream

¼ oz (7 g) vanilla

7 oz (200 g) white chocolate chunks

11 oz (310 g) frozen raspberries

1 beaten egg

Preheat oven to 375°F (190°C). In a bowl, mix flour, sugar, baking powder and salt together. Rub in butter cubes, mixing until small lumps of butter are obtained.

In a separate bowl, mix together eggs, cream and vanilla.

Add egg mixture into dry ingredients, along with white chocolate chunks. Mix just until dough starts to come together. Divide dough into 4 equal portions.

Press 1 portion of dough into a greased parchment paper–lined 8 inch (20 cm) round cake pan. Press half of frozen raspberries onto dough. Press a second portion of dough on top of the raspberries. Bang layered dough out of pan and cut into 8 wedges.

Repeat with remaining dough and raspberries.

Put scones on a parchment paper–lined baking sheet and brush with beaten egg. Bake for 20 to 25 minutes until deep golden.

Try using fresh raspberries or other fresh berries when they are in season.

Spiced Pumpkin Crème Brûlée

Serves 8

2 cups (500 mL) heavy cream

2 tsp (10 mL) brandy

1 $\frac{1}{3}$ cup (325 mL) granulated sugar, divided

$\frac{1}{4}$ tsp (1 mL) cinnamon

$\frac{1}{4}$ tsp (1 mL) ground ginger

$\frac{1}{8}$ tsp (0.5 mL) nutmeg

8 egg yolks

1 cup (250 mL) pumpkin purée

Preheat oven to 325°F (160°C). In a small saucepan, warm cream and brandy together.

In a bowl, mix $\frac{1}{3}$ cup (75 mL) sugar, cinnamon, ginger and nutmeg together. Whisk in eggs and pumpkin.

Slowly pour warm liquid from saucepan into bowl while mixing until evenly mixed. Strain mixture and cool in fridge.

Put eight 6 oz (170 g) ramekins in a rimmed baking pan and pour 1 inch (2.5 cm) water in bottom of pan. Fill ramekins $\frac{3}{4}$ full with pumpkin custard mixture. Place entire pan in oven and bake for about 30 minutes until edges are set and centres are slightly jiggly.

Remove pan and take ramekins out of water bath. Allow to cool and then refrigerate for at least 2 hours.

Liberally sprinkle surface of each ramekin with granulated sugar and then caramelize sugar using a mini blowtorch. If you haven't got a blowtorch, broil in oven for 2 to 3 minutes until sugar is caramelized.

Apple Mascarpone Cheese Torte

Serves 8 to 10

Crust

1 cup (250 mL) butter, room temperature

3½ oz (100 g) granulated sugar

11 oz (310 g) all-purpose flour

½ tsp (2 mL) vanilla

Filling

1 kg (500 g) mascarpone cheese

3½ oz (100 g) sugar

2 eggs

1 tsp (5 mL) vanilla

2 Tbsp (30 mL) Calvados (apple liqueur)

Topping

½ cup (125 mL) brown sugar

½ cup (125 mL) rolled oats

2 tsp (10 mL) cinnamon

4 Granny Smith apples, peeled and sliced

Preheat oven to 350°F (175°C). Cream butter and sugar together until light. Mix in flour and vanilla, mixing until fully combined. Press dough into base and halfway up sides of a greased 10 inch (25 cm) springform pan. Bake for 25 to 30 minutes until golden. Do not remove from pan; allow to cool.

For filling, beat mascarpone cheese with sugar until smooth. Scrape down bowl. Beat in eggs 1 at a time. Scrape down bowl. Add vanilla and Calvados. Pour filling on top of cooled, baked crust still in springform pan.

For topping, mix brown sugar, oats and cinnamon together. Fan out sliced apples on top of filling and then sprinkle with topping.

Bake for another 50 to 60 minutes until apples are tender and filling is set.

Dark Chocolate Espresso Mousse with Raspberries

Makes 10

½ cup (125 mL) espresso

¼ cup (60 mL) Kahlua

10 ladyfingers, cut in half widthwise

9 oz (255 g) dark chocolate couverture (58% to 70%)

3 egg yolks

1 oz (28 g) granulated sugar

⅓ cup (75 mL) 2% milk

⅓ cup (75 mL) heavy cream

2 cups (500 mL) heavy cream, whipped to soft peaks

1 basket fresh raspberries

1 cup (250 mL) white chocolate shavings

1 Tbsp (15 mL) cocoa powder

Mix espresso and Kahlua together. Dip each ladyfinger half into liquid and then place 2 pieces in each of 10 martini glasses. Set aside.

Melt dark chocolate couverture.

In a small saucepan, mix egg yolks and sugar together. Whisk in milk and first amount of cream. Cook over medium, stirring constantly, until mixture coats back of a spoon. Immediately pour over melted dark chocolate. Whisk until smooth. Allow to cool to lukewarm.

Fold in whipped cream. Spoon mousse over ladyfingers in martini glasses. Place in refrigerator to set.

To serve, allow mousse to come to room temperature. Garnish with fresh raspberries, white chocolate shavings and a dusting of cocoa powder.

Meringue Nests with Lemon Curd and Strawberries

Serves 8

Meringue

3½ oz (100 g) egg whites

6 oz (170 g) granulated sugar

¼ oz (7 g) cornstarch

1 tsp (5 mL) white vinegar

Lemon Curd

zest from 3 lemons

1 cup (250 mL) sugar

1 vanilla bean, split and scraped

4 eggs

¾ cup (175 mL) lemon juice

¾ cup (175 mL) cubed, cold butter

Strawberries

2 Tbsp (30 mL) sugar

1 vanilla bean, split and scraped

1 basket strawberries, hulled and sliced

Preheat oven to 250°F (120°C). Whip egg whites until soft peaks form. Gradually add sugar, whipping until stiff peaks form. Fold in cornstarch and vinegar.

Spoon large mounds of meringue on a parchment paper–lined baking sheet and then create an indentation in centre of each meringue. Bake for 50 minutes, then turn off oven, open door slightly and leave in for another 60 minutes.

Store nests in an airtight container at room temperature.

For lemon curd, rub lemon zest, sugar and vanilla bean together in a bowl. Whisk in eggs and lemon juice. Cook in a double boiler, stirring constantly, until custard thickens. Strain into a food processor and mix in butter gradually. Refrigerate curd, covered, to set.

Rub sugar and vanilla bean together. Remove vanilla pod and reserve for another use. Toss sliced strawberries with vanilla sugar.

To serve, place a spoonful of lemon curd in centre of meringue nests and top with strawberries.

Salted Caramel Ice Cream

Makes 4 cups (1 L)

¾ cup (175 mL) granulated sugar

3 Tbsp (45 mL) water

9 egg yolks

1 tsp (5 mL) salt

1⅔ cups (400 mL) 2% milk

1⅔ cups (400 mL) heavy cream

1 vanilla bean, split and scraped

In a small saucepan, stir sugar and water. Cook over medium-high until dark caramel in colour. Immediately pour caramel onto a piece of parchment and let set.

Grind set caramel into a powder using a food processor. Mix powder with egg yolks and salt; set aside.

In a medium saucepan, heat milk, cream and vanilla bean. Once liquid is hot, whisk a third of it into egg yolk mixture. Then pour everything back into saucepan.

Cook over medium, stirring constantly, until custard coats back of a spoon. Immediately strain into a bowl and chill over an ice bath.

Allow to cool completely before churning in an ice cream machine according to manufacturer's directions.

About Culinary Team Canada

Roger Andrews

Roger is a member of Team Canada and a chef instructor in the Culinary Arts Program at the College of the North Atlantic in St. John's, Newfoundland & Labrador. Roger won first prize at the 2010 Cream International Chowder Championship and placed second in 2007, 2009 and 2010 at the highly regarded International PEI Shellfish Chef Challenge.

Recipes Contributed: Fried Clams with Avocado Dip; Land and Sea Chowder; Serrano Ham-wrapped Cod Loin with Split Pea Purée; Lobster and Chanterelle Risotto.

Serge Belair

Serge is a member of Team Canada. He was born and raised in the small town of Gatineau, Québec. Since 2005, he has worked at the Shaw Conference Centre in Edmonton, where he holds the position of Senior Sous Chef.

Poyan Danesh

Poyan is a member of Team Canada, Culinary Development Chef for Frobisher International and chef of Culinary Vision, his own catering and consulting company. Previously he was Chef de Partie at Pear Tree Restaurant in Vancouver and placed fourth in Global TV's Season 1 series *The Next Great Chef*. His first international gold medal came as a Team Canada supporting member at the 2006 Luxembourg competition.

Recipes Contributed: BC Albacore Tuna Tataki with Watercress, Endive and

Grapefruit Salad and Ponzu Dressing; BC Spot Prawn Salad with Baby Spinach, Arugula and Shaved Fennel with Wasabi Vinaigrette; Braised Vancouver Island Beef Short Ribs with Natural Reduction; Braised Local Lamb Shanks, Lentil Ragout and Buttered Fava Beans; Herb-roasted Polderside Farms Chicken, Roasted Baby Nugget Potatoes with Bacon, Glazed French Beans and Tomato Jam; Hazelnut-crusted Chilliwack Trout with Sweet Pea Risotto and Pea Froth.

Peter Dewar

Peter is a member of Team Canada and a Culinary Arts Chef Instructor at Nova Scotia Community College (NSCC) in Kentville. Peter won the CATCH seafood competition in 2010, first prize in the CCFCC National Chefs Challenge in 2008, and the International PEI Shellfish Chef Challenge in 2007 and 2008.

Recipes Contributed: Mussel Soup with Avocado, Tomato and Cilantro; Asparagus Vichyssoise with Tarragon; Seared Halibut with Arugula, Roasted Beets and Horseradish Mayonnaise; Seared Tuna with Nova Scotia Hodge Podge; Sweet Pea and Lobster Lasagna; Soba Noodles with Asparagus, Digby Scallops and Sweet Miso Sauce.

Clayton Folkers

Clayton is a coach of Team Canada and a baking instructor in the School of Hospitality and Culinary Arts at the Northern Alberta Institute of Technology in Edmonton. Clayton has garnered many culinary awards since he began competing in 1978. In both individual and team competition, he has repeatedly shown a creativity and originality that has placed him at the top of his field. His expertise was acknowledged in 1991 when Clayton became the first Canadian-born chef ever appointed to a Canadian national culinary team.

Patrick Gayler

Patrick is a member of Team Canada and Executive Sous Chef at the Inn at Laurel Point in Victoria. Previously, Pat was Saucier, then Sous Chef, then Dining Room Chef at Catch Restaurant in Calgary. He was recognized as Apprentice of the Year in 2004.

Recipes Contributed: Fresh Fanny Bay Oysters with Double-smoked Bacon and Shallot Vinaigrette; Seared Qualicum Scallops with Fennel and Golden Beet Salad with Grapefruit; Sloping Hills Organic Bone-in Pork Loin with Risotto; Sidney Island Rack of Venison with Saanich Blueberry Glaze; Thyme Butter-baked Sockeye Salmon with Buttered Spaetzle, Sautéed Pearl Onions and Chanterelle Mushrooms; Grilled Haida Gwaii Halibut with Citrus Ricotta Gnocchi and Cherry Tomato Caper Ragout.

James Holehouse

James is a member and Pastry Chef of Team Canada. He became the Executive Pastry Chef at the Shaw Conference Centre in Edmonton in 2007 at the age of 28.

Recipes Contributed: White Chocolate Raspberry Scones; Spiced Pumpkin Crème Brûlée; Apple Mascarpone Cheese Torte; Dark Chocolate Espresso Mousse with Raspberries; Meringue Nests with Lemon Curd and Strawberries; Salted Caramel Ice Cream.

Brad Horen

Brad is captain of Team Canada. In 2007, Brad won the CCFCC National Chefs Challenge and represented Canada at the WACS Global Chefs Challenge in Florida.

Recipes Contributed: Salt and Pepper Squid with Togarashi Dip; Barbecued Duck Consommé; Braised Chuck Flat Stroganoff; Choucroute; Gnocchi with Wild Mushrooms and Duck Confit; Poached Pickerel with a Ragout of Clams, Mussels and Spot Prawns.

Bruno Marti, CCC

Bruno is a coach of Team Canada and Chef and Owner of La Belle Auberge Restaurant in Ladner, BC. La Belle Auberge Restaurant was awarded the Zagat Vancouver Guide Best Food Award in 2010. Bruno is the recipient of the Order of British Columbia and the Queen's Jubilee Award, and has been inducted into the BC Restaurant Hall of Fame and the American Culinary Federation. Bruno was the CFCC Chef of the Year in 1997 and was a member of the first Canadian team in history to win gold at the World Culinary Olympics in 1984.

Recipes Contributed: Pork Belly with Creamy Polenta; Roasted Duck with Blueberry Sauce; Smoked Salmon with Phyllo Crust.

Restituto Mendoza

Restituto is the assistant manager of Team Canada and Executive Chef at Pinebrook Golf and Country Club in Calgary. Restituto has competed with four teams at the Culinary Olympics.

Dave Ryan

Dave is a member of Team Canada and a Culinary Arts Instructor at Vancouver Community College. In 2010, he was honoured as the CCFCC BC Chef of the Year. For his contribution to education, Dave was awarded the 2008 Julius Pokomandy Award by Vancouver Community College.

Recipes Contributed: Baked Baby Tomato, Basil and Goat Cheese Tart with Aged Balsamico; Corn Butter Lobster Stew; Olive Oil-poached Salmon Soup with Baby Vegetables and Tomato Chutney; Bacon-wrapped Chicken Breast with Creamy Roasted Corn Polenta; BC Spot Prawn and Wild Salmon Cakes with Firecracker Rice and Kaffir Lemongrass Sauce.

Simon Smotkowicz, CCC

Simon is the business manager of Team Canada and Executive Chef at the Shaw Conference Centre in Edmonton. He was a member of Team Canada when it won the World Culinary Olympics in Germany in 1992 and was managing the team when it twice won the World Championship title at ScotHot. In 1998, Simon was selected CCFCC National Chef of the Year.

Recipes Contributed: Roasted Beef Tenderloin in a Box; Marinated Rack of Lamb with Honey Pumpkin Seed Crust and Inniskillin Merlot Essence; Pan-seared Scallops and Ragout of Summer Vegetables in a Phyllo Pastry Frying Pan with Minted Orange Sauce; Fairwinds Goat Cheese Soufflé.

Vinod Varshney

Vinod is manager of Culinary Team Alberta and Program Head of the School of Hospitality and Culinary Arts at the Northern Alberta Institute of Technology in Edmonton.

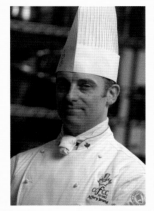

Jeffery Young

Jeffery is a member of Team Canada and Culinary Development Chef for Browns Restaurant Group in Vancouver. He won the 2009 BC Chefs Association's Chef of the Year competition. Jeffery won a gold medal at the 2002 Las Vegas Culinary Challenge.

Recipes Contributed: Pacific Dungeness Crab and Chive Soufflé Cakes with Ricotta and Citrus; Wild Mushroom and Goat Cheese Ravioli with Arugula and Red Pepper Relish; Fraser Valley Pork Tenderloin, Okanagan Sour Apple and Port Wine Caramel, Yam Purée, Spinach and Crispy Onion Rings; Natural Venison Meat Loaf with Double-smoked Bacon and Krause Farms Wild Blackberry and Red Wine Sauce; Rossdown Farm Roasted Chicken Breast with Garlic and Thyme Potatoes, Red Onion Marmalade and Pan Jus; Maple Vanilla-cured Wild BC Sockeye Salmon with Green Pea Purée and Krause Farms Blueberry and Bourbon Butter.

Fred Zimmerman, CCC

Fred is a coach of Team Canada and an international culinary judge. He captained Team Canada to a World Culinary Olympics championship in 1992. If a patriarch exists among Canadian chefs, it is Fred Zimmerman. With over 40 years of experience in the foodservice industry, Fred's guidance and leadership have benefited not only Culinary Team Canada but also many chefs in their individual professional development.

Additional recipes contributed by:

Tim Appleton: Cream of Wild Rice Soup; Great Northern White Bean Soup with Gorgonzola; Spiced Pork Tenderloin with Leek and Apple Cider Sauce and a Pear and Raisin Chutney; Seared Walleye on Creamed Fennel with Tomato Confit.

Arthur Chen: Brioche.

Cameron Huley: Manitoba Corn Soup; Crabapple and Brussels Sprouts Salad; Buckwheat Honey-roasted Duck with Pumpkin Risotto; Pan-roasted Pheasant Breast with Saskatoon Berry Jus.

Marcel Kretz, CCC: Tortilla Rolls with Cream Cheese, Walnuts and Olives; Olive Bread; Chicken, Savoy Cabbage and Barley Soup; Québec Meat Pie with Game and Mushrooms; Alsatian Onion Tart.

Christophe Luzeux, CCC: White Asparagus Soup; Veal Chops with Morel Sauce; Flamish Chicken in Dark Beer; Dover Sole "Meuniere"-style with Capers.

Jud Simpson: Buttercup Squash Velour; Makkhani Murhi (Chicken in Butter Sauce).

Index